To my sons Jacen and Benjamin

BAPTIZED INTO CHRIST

A Guide to the Christian Life

BAPTIZED INTO CHRIST: A GUIDE TO THE
CHRISTIAN LIFE
BY JORDAN COOPER

Just & Sinner
425 East Lincoln Ave.
Watseka, IL 60970

www.JustandSinner.com

ISBN 10: 0692699341
ISBN 13: 978-0692699348

TABLE OF CONTENTS

INTRODUCTION

If you walk into your local Christian bookstore, you will see a lot of books about the Christian life. But what you won't find are books that talk about Christian living from a uniquely Lutheran perspective. As Lutherans, we are proficient in releasing theological literature, and excel at proclaiming the gospel of free grace in Jesus Christ. But many people in our pews are left asking: "What does this mean for me during the week? How do I live out my life as a Christian each day?" This book is an attempt to bring Lutheran theology to a level that is both understandable to the average reader, and practical.

My previous writing has mostly been academic, aimed at theologians, pastors, and those who have studied the basics of Christian theology. This work is an attempt to bring the study and writing I have done elsewhere down to a level that the average Christian is able to understand. It is my hope that this book will be a helpful resource for church Bible studies and something that any Christian can benefit from.

The Christian life is an immensely important topic. Ultimately, it's the most important aspect of Christian doctrine, because all of theology should have the goal of impacting the life of the average Christian. Each topic in this volume could easily be a book of its own. At the end of each chapter, I have included resources for further reading that you can look at if you want to further research each topic. My hope is that this work will edify you, causing you to cling evermore strongly to Christ, and walk with him in love toward one another.

Jordan Cooper
Watseka, IL
2016

CHAPTER 1

DISCOVERING YOUR BAPTISMAL IDENTITY

Identity is a concept that is often discussed in our culture, but no one seems to understand it. Everyone is on a search for it, but no one can find it. People talk about "finding themselves." This has left us in a cultural dilemma, where no one knows who they are, and people seem to think that they will somehow stumble upon their identity as long as they search long enough, and hard enough. The shocking answer to this search for meaning and identity is that you won't find it. Your identity isn't to be found in what your interests are, who you are friends with, or what your personality is like. Contrary to what popular culture might tell you, if you have problems in your marriage, they won't be solved by stepping away from it and experimenting, finding out who "you" really are. This experiment will, in fact, only worsen the problem.

We have all had times of identity crisis in our lives. At least on occasion, we all wonder about who and what we are. I remember in high school, being so tied to my first long-term girlfriend that I did not know who I was apart from that relationship. We dated for about a year and a half, and seemingly out of nowhere— she dumped me. I was devastated. Break ups are always hard; everyone who has gone through a difficult breakup can relate to such feelings. This is especially true for a teenager with unstable emotions and raging hormones. I was a mess. I didn't know who I was without her, because I based my entire identity on my relationship with this girl. So I quickly jumped into a couple other short relationships because I thought that this would somehow solve the problem. It shouldn't come as a surprise that this didn't actually resolve anything. I was still left wondering about my identity.

I also often struggled finding my identity in the things I was interested in. For example—I'm kind of a nerd. Ok, that's an understatement. I am a huge geek. I love science fiction, and especially the Star Wars saga. I don't just mean that I've seen the movies a few times and enjoy them. I've read just about all of the novels (somewhere around 130), and many of the comics. As a teenager, my entire bedroom was filled with Star Wars collectibles. If you ask my wife, she'll tell you that she almost ran away the first time she visited my parents' house and saw my collection. She thought I was a little obsessive—which very well may be the truth. I still have an entire room in my house dedicated to my Star Wars collectibles. Anyway, that was one of those things I was known for. I had a huge collection of Star Wars memorabilia. Because of that, it was easy for me to find my identity in that particular interest of mine. That was something that differentiated me from other people. I was the nerdy guy who loved Star Wars, and had a big collection.

I realize now that both of these things I did were wrong. I couldn't identify myself by who my current girlfriend was, or by what my interests were. It only brought confusion about my true self. The problem with the way that we approach this subject is that we are always looking inside ourselves to find some kind of "self" that we can identify with, or need to discover. But this is precisely the problem. Our identity is not to be found in ourselves. It is to be found in something— some*one* rather—outside of us. Your identity is not to be found in your boyfriend, girlfriend, or spouse. It's not to be found in your particular quirks, interests, or career. Your identity is to be found in the one who redeemed you, the one who gave up his own life for your sin, the one who places his very name on you when you are baptized. Your identity is found in Christ.

Who you are: A Sinner

If you search through the self-help section of your local bookstore, you probably aren't going to find many books about sin or repentance. Instead, you will find books pointing you inward. The message you will hear is: You are wonderful and special in and of yourself, and you can do great things if you only try! We are all like the little engine that could. If we just tell ourselves that we can accomplish whatever we want, then we can!

This way of thinking about ourselves is not new. In the fifth century, a British monk named Pelagius taught something very similar to what we find in contemporary self-help resources. He argued that humanity is not, by nature, sinful. Instead, we are all born into this world in a neutral state. We are innocent from the womb, and our lives are then governed by our individual choices. Yes, it is true that most people choose sin, but we don't *have* to. Instead, by our own will-power, we can choose to be good and righteous. We can pull ourselves up by our own bootstraps. A man named Augustine of Hippo received some criticism from Pelagius, because Augustine believed that all people are sinful from birth. Augustine wrote against Pelagius' teaching because it went against the clear words of Scripture. According to God's Word, people aren't born naturally good, or morally neutral. Instead, Scripture tells us that we are conceived in sin (Psalm 51:5), and that we are spiritually dead from birth (Eph. 2:5). Pelagius taught that Adam's sin does not make us sinful by nature. Instead, it simply serves as a bad example that we can avoid, should we make the right decisions. If we do sin, we can simply do more and try harder, and save ourselves (with some help from God of course). Augustine taught, along with the Apostle Paul, that through Adam's sin, all are made sinners. Because of that, no human being has the power to save themselves.

We don't like to think of ourselves as bad people. We *really* don't like to talk about sin—well, at least not our own. All of us naturally think like Pelagius. We want to believe that salvation comes from our own hands. We don't want to admit how desperate for grace we really are. It's one thing to admit that we make mistakes *sometimes*, but it's another to really acknowledge that our very core is sinful. Who wants to hear that? But the truth is, if we want to discover who we really are, if we want to find our identity in this world, we need to be honest with ourselves. If we aren't honest with ourselves about our sin, then we will continue our path of self-deception. When we try to find our identity inside of ourselves, and place our worth in who we are and what we have done, we are putting on a mask. It's like getting into a car accident and severely damaging every part of your face, and then walking around with a mask trying to convince yourself that this mask defines what you really look like. Deep down, you always know that you are in fact wearing a mask, no matter how much you try to convince yourself otherwise. In the same way, when you try and find your worth within yourself, you are putting on the mask of goodness, trying really hard to convince yourself that you *really are good*, and that your sin doesn't exist. But deep down, you know that you have a problem. You know that you are a sinner.

Your Identity in Christ

Thankfully, you don't have to look for your identity within yourself. Be honest, and acknowledge that hope will never be found within your own actions. Instead, look to the identity which God has placed upon you in Holy Baptism. Your worth is not found within yourself, but in Christ.

When you were baptized, life-changing words were spoken by the minister. These words do not arise from church tradition; it's not a nice sentimental act to remind you of a salvation given somewhere else. The words of God are profound. They are earth-shattering. "I baptize you in the name of the Father, the Son, and the Holy Spirit." You are baptized in a *name*. The name which you are baptized into is not your own, and it isn't the name of the pastor baptizing you, or the person who brought you to faith. Instead, it is the very name of *God himself*. So what exactly does this mean? Why has God baptized you in his own name, and what does this have to do with your identity? By being baptized in the name of the Triune God, you are being identified *with* the Triune God. You do not need to find you worth or value within yourself, but in him.

A helpful illustration of what that means can be found in Paul's first letter to the Corinthians. He writes that "our fathers were all under the cloud, and all passed through the sea, and all were baptized into Moses in the cloud and in the sea" (1 Cor. 10:1-2). Paul refers to the

Exodus in this text. The Exodus is one of the most famous events in Biblical history, where God rescues the people of Israel from their bondage in the land of Egypt. He does this by using Moses as his spokesperson. And through this man, God worked all sorts of miracles which led to their escape from the Egyptians, and their eventual arrival in the Promised Land. But in this whole story, as we read it in the book of Exodus, there is no mention of baptism. So why does Paul connect what Moses does to baptism? This seems to be rather out of place.

If you know anything about the story of Israel, you know that God's people were not always the most obedient children of their Heavenly Father. This was true in Moses' time, as well as throughout the rest of the history of Israel. In fact, this is true today of the church as well. But thankfully, God did not rescue Israel based on their merits or worthiness. If he did that, they would never pass the test. There were many who strongly believed in the God who was delivering them, and others went along for the ride just because they wanted to get out of slavery. Yet, God delivered them all anyway. This is where we get to the point that Paul makes. God chose one particular man to lead the people out of Egypt—Moses. Now, he was certainly not a sinless man, as is evident throughout the Biblical narrative, but he was a representative of God, and being that representative, he was righteous. It was Moses who had the power, given by God, to perform miracles. He was the one who opened up the Red Sea, and in doing so, all the people were delivered along with him. The people of Israel were saved in the Exodus *because they were identified with God's representative*—Moses. This is what Paul means when saying that the people were "baptized into Moses." They were identified with him, and being identified with him, they partook of God's salvation. In the same way, we are identified with Christ, who is the ultimate representative of the Father. And by baptism, we are identified with him and his act of redemption on the cross.

The language of being baptized "into Christ" is used quite a bit in the New Testament. In Galatians 3:27, Paul writes, "As many of you as were baptized into Christ have put on Christ." Though some Christian traditions teach that baptism does not actually *do* anything, and that this verse is referring to Spirit baptism instead of water baptism (a distinction that Scripture does not make), there is no reason to assume that the verse means anything other than what it says. When you are baptized, something actually *happens*—something profound. You are placed into Christ Jesus. You are connected with him and everything that he has becomes yours. Martin Luther describes this wonderful act of God as a marriage between the Christian and his Savior. The believer is connected to Jesus like a man and his wife are connected in marriage, only the bond of Jesus and the Christian is even deeper. In a marriage, the husband and wife share everything that belongs to them with the other person. This is what Jesus does when we are connected to him. He takes all that is ours (our sin and brokenness), and gives us what is his (his life and righteousness). Though we cannot define ourselves simply by our human relationships, we can define who we are by this relationship to Christ. In it, he gives us his own worth and value, so that we do not have to look within ourselves to find it.

Baptism: It's God's Work

Most Christians will agree that baptism is something very important in the Christian life, but many Christians disagree about the nature and meaning of the sacrament. In many modern churches, baptism is viewed as an act of human obedience. We are saved by God's grace, and after his grace is received, we must respond to God in obedience. We do this by being baptized. This ordinance is a public act through which we confess our faith before the world. This view leads to a rejection of infant baptism due to the fact that an infant is not at an appropriate age to make such a decision.

There is an important question which must be asked when we are discussing baptism, because it defines how we look at our baptismal identity. Is baptism the work of man, or is it the work of God? If baptism is the work of man—if it is something the Christian is supposed to do in order to obey God's will—then it will not serve as a grounds for our assurance in

Christ. In that approach, baptism cannot be anything but a symbol because we know that we are not saved by human works (Eph. 2:8-9). If this is true, then how can we look to baptism for our identity in Christ? If baptism is a work of man, then we are again pushed back on ourselves to define who we really are before God. This approach to baptism, which is taught by many Baptist and non-denominational churches, is not taught in Scripture.

Let's look at some passages that talk about the meaning and purpose of baptism.

And Peter said to them, "Repent and be baptized every one of you in the name of Jesus Christ for the forgiveness of your sins, and you will receive the gift of the Holy Spirit. (Acts 2:38)

This is one of the clearest verses about baptism in the New Testament, which comes from the sermon given by Peter at Pentecost. In the context, Peter is preaching to a group of Jews who came together from all over the world to celebrate the feast of Pentecost. He stood up in front of all of these people to teach them that Jesus had come as the messiah, and that he had been killed under Jewish hands. We are told that those listening had been "cut to the heart," and ask Peter the question: "What shall we do" (Acts 2:37)? These people were struck by the guilt of their sin. They realized that they had rejected and killed the messiah who was sent to save them. And in response to their guilt, they asked Peter the question: "What shall we do?" They wanted Peter to give them a solution to their guilt problem. They recognized themselves as sinners, and they needed salvation! That gift of salvation is exactly what Peter offered them. He told them that the forgiveness of sins would be theirs if only they would repent and be baptized! Baptism does not come to these Jews as a word of law, as an extra commandment that they need to check off their list of good works. Rather, it is a word of gospel! It's a word of hope, that God would use the waters of baptism to wash away their sins!

Baptism, which corresponds to this, now saves you, not as a removal of dirt from the body but as an appeal to God for a good conscience, through the resurrection of Jesus Christ. (1 Peter 3:21)

As a Lutheran pastor, probably the most common objections I get from other Christians regarding my beliefs are on the topic of baptism. Many Christians argue that baptism is a work, and Scripture is clear that we are not saved by works. Therefore, it is argued, baptism cannot save. But like every theological argument, we have a duty to test this claim by Scripture, and the Apostle Peter says exactly this—Baptism now saves you! This quote comes from a discussion about the flood which occurred at the time of Noah. In this stage of redemptive history, humankind had become severely corrupt, and God decided that he was going to destroy the earth with a flood. He did not will the utter destruction of the human race, however, but he decided to save one family. God chose to save Noah and his relatives who would then repopulate the earth. As the rain waters began to pour down onto the earth, Noah climbed up upon the ark with his family, and through it they were saved from the flood waters. Their lives were spared.

Peter tells us that the flood was a picture of baptism. There are two parallels that are clear between the flood and baptism—First, both are instances where God uses water. In the flood, God cleansed the earth from evil and saved Noah and his family. In the waters of baptism, God places his name on us and brings us into his family. Second, they are both instances of salvation. In the flood, God saved Noah and his family from destruction. In baptism, God saves us from guilt and death. If Peter did not believe that baptism actually saved people, he would not speak in this way.

Some people try and argue that the fact that Peter says "not as a removal of dirt from the body" means that he is not referring to water baptism. But that misses the point entirely. What Peter means here is that baptism saves, but it does not save just as some kind of external washing. Rather, it saves because *God has attached his promise to it.* God's Word works with the water, so that through it he cleanses your conscience. This is such an important point—baptism cleanses your conscience! It good-consciences you! The search for identity is in many ways a search for a clean conscience. We know that we have messed up in our lives. We have guilt, and shame. In our search for our identity we turn to vices, or virtues to hide this guilt. We look to our own works, our own performance. But before God, your identity is not found in your performance. It is found in who you are in Christ. You are God's baptized child, and because of that you have a clean conscience!

Living the Baptismal Life

The entire life of the Christian is essentially summed up by the act of baptism. Here, God declares you to be righteous in him. He declares that you belong to him, and that you are his child. We must hold onto this, not simply as an event that happened many years in the past, but as a daily reality. We should be daily reminding ourselves of our baptism, because by doing that, we remind ourselves of our true identity.

When we speak about our baptism, we should not simply say, "I *was* baptized," but instead we should say, "I *am* baptized." Baptism is not just an event of the past, but it's something that affects you every day of your life. You *are* a baptized Christian. This is why Martin Luther recommended using the sign of the cross. We often think of the sign of the cross as some kind of Roman Catholic ritual, but it is much more than that. By making the sign of the cross over ourselves, we remember who we are according to our baptisms. You were baptized into the name of the Father, the Son, and the Holy Spirit. When making the sign of the cross, Christians repeat those same words to themselves as a reminder of who they belong to. Every morning when you wake up, make the sign of the cross over yourself. Let it serve as a reminder to you throughout the day of your identity in Christ.

Resources for Further Reading:

Das, A. Andrew. *Baptized into God's Family: The Doctrine of Infant Baptism for Today.* Milwaukee: Northwestern, 1997.

Gerberding, George Henry. *The Way of Salvation in the Lutheran Church.* American Lutheran Classics Vol. 1. Fairfield, IA: Just and Sinner, 2013, 31-42.

Mueller, Steven P. *Called to Believe, Teach, and Confess: An Introduction to Doctrinal Theology.* Eugene: Wipf & Stock, 2005, 329-346.

Saarnivaara, Uuras *Scriptural Baptism: a Dialog Between John Bapstead and Martin Childfont.* New York: Vantage Press, 1953.

Scaer, David P. *Baptism.* Confessional Lutheran Dogmatics Vol. XI. St. Louis: Luther Academy, 1999.

CHAPTER 2

THE TWO KINDS OF RIGHTEOUSNESS

Everyone lives with different types of relationships. I am a husband, but I am also a pastor and a father. Each of these relationships differs from the others. I have a different kind of relationship with my wife than I do with my son, or with my congregants, or with the man who delivers my mail. But among all the varied relationships we have, there are essentially *two kinds* of relationships. First, there are these human relationships, which, though they vary, are all based in *some sense* upon how we live. The way that we act and treat one another will affect how we get along with one another. Second, there is a relationship with God. All people are in some kind of relationship with God. Whether people want to acknowledge it or not, God is the Creator of all, and no one can escape his presence. Those who have not repented, and do not believe, have a negative relationship to God. Refusing to acknowledge him as God, they seek to establish their creaturely identity on their own. In contrast to these individuals, there are Christians. These are those who have faith in Jesus Christ and who repent of their sins. They have a *positive* relationship with God. God loves his people, he desires to grant them all good gifts and blessings. The relationship we have with God differs, in a variety of ways, from the relationships that we have with one another.

Our Relationship with God: Passive Righteousness

God has, from the time of creation, desired to be the giver of gifts to the people that he has made. He delights in self-giving. God created us, and not we ourselves. He made us apart from any creaturely decision, and solely as a gift of his own free grace. Following the event of creation, God provided Adam all that he needed for bodily life in the Garden. God gave him food, direction as to how to live, a job, and a wife. Adam was called to live before God as one who simply received God's good gifts. He was not called to earn anything, but to live in the relationship that God's grace that was already established. God's love was not a result of Adam's worthiness or merit. Grace alone is the cause of God's love.

The fall of man profoundly affected the relationship between the Creator and his creation. Brokenness and sin entered the world through Adam's failure to obey God's will. However, despite our sin, God's fundamental attitude toward man has remained the same. He wants us to live not as self-sufficient beings, but as those who owe our very breath to the Creator. God does not call us to earn his favor by our own efforts. When we do this, we rob God of his role as gracious giver and merciful redeemer. We put ourselves in his place, attempting to establish identity by our own deeds. God wants us to come before him, not as people who *do*, but as people who *receive*. He desires our acknowledgement that he is God and that we are not. We do this, not by thinking we have anything sufficient to offer a holy God, but by opening our empty hands of faith and receiving what he desires to give.

Martin Luther described the relationship that Christians have with God as one of passive righteousness. Our righteousness before God is not something we can earn. We do not try our best in order that God will reward us with salvation. In fact, if we live in that way, we endanger our salvation! This is a rejection of the redemption that God offers through his own work and grace. Our righteousness before God is instead a passive righteousness. We cannot do anything to earn this righteousness; God desires to give it to us as a free gift of his grace! Our relationship before God, then, is a passive one. As we will discuss below, this relationship differs greatly from relationships we have with our fellow human beings.

Along with "passive righteousness," Martin Luther used a variety of terms to describe God's righteousness which saves sinners. One of these terms is "alien righteousness." Despite what the modern reader might assume, Luther did not mean by that term that we need to get our righteousness from Wookiees or Klingons, but that our righteousness comes from an outside source. Due to the Fall, we lack goodness and righteousness. Sin is part of our identity from conception, and thus true righteousness cannot be found within. Instead, we need to find a righteousness from somewhere else. Our righteousness is found in God, and is granted as a gift.

This concept of righteousness was at the heart of the Protestant Reformation. In the medieval church, Luther was taught that his righteousness before God, in some sense, consisted in his own works. Knowing the reality of his sin, Luther feared the phrase "the righteousness of God." Rather than the righteousness which delivers and redeems, he believed that "the righteousness of God," consisted of God's judgment toward sinners. Luther understood the truth that he broke God's commandments each day of his life. While preparing to teach from book of Romans, Luther pondered the phrase "the righteousness of God," which St. Paul uses throughout this epistle. Through his reading of Paul and St. Augustine, Martin Luther made a revolutionary discovery. This righteousness of God that Paul speaks about is not simply that righteousness by which God *himself* is righteous. Rather, God's righteousness is a gift that he gives to sinners! Writing about his experience studying St. Paul, Luther writes:

I began to understand that this verse [Rom. 1:16-17] means that the justice of God is revealed through the Gospel, but it is a passive justice, i.e. that by which the merciful God justifies us by faith, as it is written: "The just person lives by faith." All at once I felt that I had been born again and entered into paradise itself through open gates. Immediately I saw the whole of Scripture in a different light. I ran through the Scriptures from memory and found that other terms had analogous meanings, e.g., the work of God, that is, what God works in us; the power of God, by which he makes us powerful; the wisdom of God, by which he makes us wise; the strength of God, the salvation of God, the glory of God.[1]

This discovery was at the core of the Reformation—sinners are saved, not by themselves, but by the gift of God.

The word which Scripture uses to explain this concept of passive righteousness is "justification." St. Paul explains in Romans writing: "One is justified by faith apart from works of the law" (Rom. 3:28).

---

[1] An Excerpt From: Preface to the Complete Edition of Luther's Latin Works (1545) by Dr. Martin Luther, 1483-1546 Translated by Bro. Andrew Thornton, OSB from the "Vorrede zu Band I der Opera Latina der Wittenberger Ausgabe. 1545" in vol. 4 of _Luthers Werke in Auswahl_, ed. Otto Clemen,6th ed., (Berlin: de Gruyter. 1967). pp. 421-428.

Justification is a word that means "to declare righteous," or "to vindicate." The Roman Catholic tradition defines the term "justification" as a process whereby the sinner gradually *becomes* righteousness. This is what Lutherans refer to as sanctification, which needs to be distinguished from justification. If our justification is some kind of renewal that happens *within* us, then we can never have assurance of our salvation. How do we ever know that we have done quite enough? How do we know that we *really* have favor with God? It is essential to understand the Biblical meaning of this term as a *declaration* that one is righteous, rather than the process whereby one is *made* righteous.

If you are justified, this means that you have been declared righteous in God's sight. When God looks upon you, he does not take any of your sin and failures into account. Instead, he looks at you as being perfectly righteous, even though, in reality, you are a sinner. This righteousness is *imputed*, or *counted* to you. This is one of the greatest truths about the Christian faith. We are declared perfectly and fully righteous in God's sight, not because of anything that we have done, but because of what Christ has done for us! This is at the heart of the gospel, and this is what defines our relationship with God.

One of the central aspects of debate between the Lutheran and Roman Catholic Church during the Reformation, which still remains a division between the two traditions today, is the relationship between faith and works in justification. Luther argued that justification is received by faith alone. Luther's opponents conceded that people were justified by faith, but they could not agree with Luther that justification happened by faith *alone*. Instead, they argued that justification is a cooperative effort between God and man. It is a process which begins with God's grace and forgiveness at holy baptism. Man then has to contribute his own merit in the process of justification, as he is gradually made more righteous. Forgiveness is not a free gift, but one has to, in some sense, earn it with his own deeds. This approach to justification leads one away from any objective assurance that they have in Christ. If my justification is up to my own efforts, how do I know that I can actually do it? How do I know that I have done enough? It removes salvation from the hands of God, and places it within the human creature. God does not want us to live in such a way! He desires to be the God who gives, not the one who receives.

How would you feel if you were in love with someone, and every time you gave them a gift, they tried to pay you back? Say a man just bought his fiancée a wedding ring, and after proposing, she immediately took out her checkbook and tried to give the man his money back. The man would likely be quite offended; the money he spent on trying to do something nice for the one he loved would then seem meaningless. This situation might sound absurd, but this is exactly what we do when we try to earn salvation with our own works. We tell God: "Thanks, but I think I'll do it on my own. I'd rather do it my way."

Our Relationship with Others: Active Righteousness

The passive righteousness of faith is a *coram Deo* reality, which is a Latin phrase meaning "before God." Our relationship to the world, or *coram mundo*, works quite a bit differently. In our human relationships, we are *not* called to be passive. We are not called simply to be receivers in this world. Rather, God wants us to be productive. He wants us to obey his commandments, and take care of the world around us. That's why he has placed us here. He calls us to various different stations in life so that we can do things which benefit the world, and help society to function. This is what is called active righteousness.

There are some crucial differences between passive righteousness and active righteousness. Both of these realities are absolutely essential in the Christian's life, but they serve different functions. Passive righteousness defines how one relates to God. God is the giver of gifts. He is our Lord and Creator, and he wants to be recognized as such. We stand before him with empty hands, receiving all that he has to give to us, and live before him in thanksgiving for granting us free salvation in Jesus Christ. Active righteousness, in contrast, defines how one relates to other people. This righteousness is not determinative for our relationship to our Creator. However, we are called to do it, not to make God love us more, but because our neighbor needs our good works, and because we delight in the will of God!

People cannot properly function in this world if one desires to live only by passive righteousness. Imagine if I got home from work, and sat down at the dinner table at night, and told me wife: "I'm done helping around the house, and I'm also done working. From now on, I'm just going to sleep in, and make you give me everything I need. You can work from now on. You can make the food, clean, and take care of the kids. At the end of the day I'll be sure to say thanks." How do you think that conversation would go? I don't think that my wife would be too happy with me! And why wouldn't she be? Because she expects certain things from me as her husband. She expects me to take care of her, to work and earn money, and to help her around the house when she needs it. She isn't being unfair in expecting those things either, because I am called to do that! It's part of my life in this world. It's my vocation as a husband and father.

There is an instance in Scripture where a certain church got confused about how life in the world functions, and the men in that congregation decided that they were not going to work anymore. Paul writes to the Thessalonians:

Now we command you, brothers, in the name of our Lord Jesus Christ, that you keep away from any brother who is walking in idleness and not in accord with the tradition that you received from us. For you yourselves know how you ought to imitate us, because we were not idle when we were with you, nor did we eat anyone's bread without paying for it, but with toil and labor we worked night and day, that we might not be a burden to any of you. It was not because we do not have that right, but to give you in ourselves an example to imitate. For even when we were with you, we would give you this command: If anyone is not willing to work, let him not eat. For we hear that some among you walk in idleness, not busy at work, but busybodies. Now such persons we command and encourage in the Lord Jesus Christ to do their work quietly and to earn their own living. (2 Thess. 3:6-12)

There were apparently some people in the Thessalonian church who believed that because they were saved, they did not have any earthly responsibilities. Their status before God in heaven meant that they didn't need to concern themselves with earthly vocations. Instead, they could just receive whatever they wanted from others, and wait for Jesus to return. After all, if our home is in heaven, what do earthly things matter anyway?

Paul has some pretty harsh words for the Thessalonians. He says that if they won't work, they also won't eat! This is the natural order of creation. God has placed us on this earth to do certain things. If God was not concerned about our lives on this earth, then he would just kill us the moment we converted to the Christian faith. But, clearly, this is not what God has done. He has left us here on this earth to do specific things. We are called to live in society, to take care of our families, and to earn money. If everyone were to give up pursuing active righteousness, then the world would no longer function. No one would grow food, pave roads, or govern society. Anarchy would ensue.

This difference between active and passive righteousness is apparent throughout Paul's letters. Often, Paul first outlines all that God has done for human redemption in Christ, and then, following this, expounds upon the nature of the Christian life. Look, for example, at the book of Ephesians. Throughout the first chapter, Paul outlines the doctrine of election (Eph. 1:3-14). This is the teaching that God has destined us for salvation in Christ before the creation of the world. In chapter two, Paul then talks about the reality of justification, that God saved us apart from any works that we have done (Eph. 2:8-9). These sections are largely in the indicative case. An indicative is a sentence that describes something which is the case. For example, I could say "your shirt is brown." That's not a command that you should get a brown shirt, or a judgment about whether or not the brown shirt looks good on you. Rather, I am simply stating something which is true. Your shirt happens to be the color brown.

In theology, indicatives are statements like, "God sent Jesus to die for you," or "you are saved in Christ." These are gospel statements, which describe what God has done for you and who you are in Christ.

In chapter four of Ephesians, Paul's tone changes. He no longer speaks primarily in the indicative case, but he begins using imperatives. An imperative is a command. It is stating, not what *is*, but what *should be*. He writes: "I therefore, a prisoner for the Lord, urge you to walk in a manner worthy of the calling to which you have been called" (Eph. 4:1). It is only in view of who the Ephesians are in Christ, that they are then to called to live as those who are in Christ. The imperatives are always based on the indicatives. The commands of God to the Christian are always based on the reality of who the believer is in Christ. The active righteousness which the believer has in the world comes through the passive righteousness that one has from God as a free gift. God gives his love freely and without merit to the Christian. That love then flows outward toward others.

The Importance of Distinguishing the Two Kinds of Righteousness

It is imperative for us to keep this distinction in mind, because when we confuse these two kinds of righteousness, the whole Christian life is misunderstood. If we focus only on passive righteousness, there are several problems which can arise. We might act like the Thessalonians, thinking that we can just sit around and do nothing with our lives because we have salvation in Christ. Since we already have salvation, what does the rest of our life matter anyway? We also might view the Christian faith as irrelevant to our everyday lives. If we think the Christian faith is only about passive righteousness, then what relevance does it have to my life at work? How does it affect my family life? Yes, the Christian faith is important regarding my relationship to God, but what does it have to do with my life in the world? The church is called, not only to preach the gospel, but to teach about ethics as explained by God's moral law.

There are even more severe errors which happen when one views their relationship to God in active righteousness terms. In the most extreme instances, one can fall into the error of the medieval church, viewing good works as necessary for justification. This leaves one in despair, without any assurance that they are actually saved. There are less severe forms of this type of approach, such as when someone is struggling with assurance, and instead of being pointed to the objective work of Christ, and God's gifts in word and sacrament, they are pointed inward. Christians might be told that the only way they can have assurance of their own salvation is by looking inward, at the nature of their good works. This too, leads a person into despair. One might also do this by saying that while good works are not necessary for one to be justified, they are necessary in order to stay in relationship with God, or to attain heaven. Good works might not bring one into the Christian faith, but they preserve one in the faith, and are ultimately a ground by which one enters into the presence of God in heaven.

Understanding the relationship between active and passive righteousness guards us from these errors. Through passive righteousness, we have complete and perfect assurance that our sins are forgiven, and that we are declared completely and perfectly holy in God's sight. Through active righteousness, we learn how to live in the world in a God-pleasing way.

Resources for Further Reading:

Arand, Charles. "Two Kinds of Righteousness as a Framework for Law and Gospel in the Apology." *Lutheran Quarterly* XV/4 (2001): 417-39.

Arand, Charles P. and Joel Biermann. "Why the Two Kinds of Righteousness?" *Concordia Journal* 33/2 (2007) 116-135.

Biermann, Joel D. *A Case for Character: Toward a Lutheran Virtue Ethics.* Minneapolis: Fortress, 2014.

Kolb, Robert. "Luther on the Two Kinds of Righteousness; Reflections on His Two-Dimensional Definition of Humanity at the Heart of His Theology." *Lutheran Quarterly* XIII/4 (1999): 449-66.

Kolb, Robert and Charles P. Arand. *The Genius of Luther's Theology: A Wittenberg Way of Thinking for the Contemporary Church.* Grand Rapids: Baker, 2008.

CHAPTER 3

GOD'S TWO WORDS

Speech is an important part of life. It's the way in which we know the thoughts of others, and how we communicate our own ideas. We tell people our needs to get what we desire, and ask questions when we need answers. Human relationships are essentially based on speech. God reveals himself in the same way that we reveal ourselves to others—through words. God too has speech, and this serves as the bridge of communication between the Creator and his creatures.

There are many different kinds of speech. Sometimes we speak in questions, for the purpose of receiving an answer from the other party. Other times we speak in requests, meaning that we have desires which we would like others to fulfill. Often, our speech is simply informational. We use our words to inform others of something that is true. While God similarly can speak in all of these different ways, there are two primary ways in which God speaks to people: words of command, and words of promise. This distinction is an essential one for understanding God's Word, and how he addresses his creatures. This is often referred to as the distinction between law and gospel.

The Law as God's Will

One of the ways in which God speaks is by giving commands. This is seen in the earliest chapters of Genesis, where God gives commandments to Adam and Eve.

Be fruitful and multiply and fill the earth and subdue it, and have dominion over the fish of the sea and over the birds of the heavens and over every living thing that moves on the earth. (Gen. 1:28)

Since the law existed before the fall of man, we know that the law is not bad. It is a good part of God's creation; as with all gifts of God, it functions in its own particular way. God gives laws to his different creatures so that his creation functions rightly. This first commandment given to Adam was not given as a means by which Adam would merit his relationship to God, but as a helpful guide for him to live properly in the world. Through the law, Adam received God's instruction that it was his role to take care of the earth and make children. Along with this positive instruction was a negative commandment; Adam was forbidden from eating of the tree of the knowledge of good and evil. God's commandments are not a result of sin, but were given before sin, and essentially served only one function—to guide man to live in this world before God and with creation.

God has law and order within himself. His nature is righteous, moral, and good. Thus God cannot lie. He cannot judge something that is immoral to be moral. He cannot act unjustly. The law that God gives to human beings is essentially a reflection of who God is in himself. The law shows who God is, and what God considers to be right and good. Again, this shows that the law is not bad, but it is in fact holy, righteous, and good.

The Law Always Accuses: God's Commandments after the Fall

God's commandments served only a positive function before the fall. They were a guide to Adam and Eve so that they might live rightly before God. But after sin came into the world, things began to change. Before the fall, humans had the ability to obey God's commandments; after the fall, this obedience is hindered by sin. The law now serves a different function. Instead of simply guiding people's lives, the law now demonstrates that we have not lived up to its demands.

In the book of Romans, the apostle Paul demonstrates the purpose of God's law within the story of human redemption. He begins his letter by demonstrating that the pagan nations had fallen far short of God's holiness. They worshiped and served created things, rather than God himself (Rom. 1:25). The Jews had not fared much better. Though they had the privilege of receiving God's law directly through Moses, they still fell short of obeying it. While the Jews knew God's law, and they had taught it well, they committed many sins against God, even while warning others about those same sins (Rom. 2:17-24). After describing the state of all people, both Jews and gentiles under the law, Paul comes to this conclusion:

Now we know that whatever the law says it speaks to those who are under the law, so that every mouth may be stopped, and the whole world may be held accountable to God. For by works of the law no human being will be justified in his sight, since through the law comes knowledge of sin. (Rom. 3:19-20)

The law does not, and *cannot* give salvation. If we were required to earn our own salvation through the law, none of us would be redeemed; all have fallen short. Instead, the law's role is to stop the mouths of sinners. Through the law, we see the reality of who we are. We see that we have *not* kept God's commandments. We are left with no excuse before God. The law's message to you is that you are guilty, and nothing you can possibly do will get you out of the mess you have put yourself in. You deserve God's punishment for all of your sin.

The law shows you your problem, but it cannot do anything get you out of it. It simply demands; it doesn't give. We can't escape the condemnation of the law by trying harder. We can't look to education as the solution, as if the more we know, the less sin will reign over us. The law shows us that there is no escape. This is one mess that we can't get ourselves out of. We need to be rescued.

The apostle Paul demonstrates this as he writes about his own experience with God's law:

Yet if it had not been for the law, I would not have known sin. For I would not have known what it is to covet if the law had not said, "You shall not covet." But sin, seizing an opportunity through the commandment, produced in me all kinds of covetousness. For apart from the law, sin lies dead. I was once alive apart from the law, but when the commandment came, sin came alive and I died. The very commandment that promised life proved to be death to me. For sin, seizing an opportunity through the commandment, deceived me and through it killed me. So the law is holy, and the commandment is holy and righteous and good. (Rom. 7:7-12)

Paul says that he was once "alive apart from the law." He isn't saying here that at one time he was without sin, but that he hadn't *realized* that he was dead in his trespasses in sins. Before hearing the law, we have high opinions of ourselves. We like to think that we are pretty good people, as if sin is no big deal. But when the law comes to us with conviction, we see the truth. The blinders are removed, and we now understand the depth of sin.

Paul mentions that it was particularly the commandment of covetousness that caused him to understand the reality of his sin. We often evaluate our own goodness by pointing to the sins of others. If you ask someone if they think they are a good person, you'll often get the answer, "Well, sure, I haven't killed anybody." We like to try and think we haven't committed those really evil sins, and those small ones don't really matter that much, do they? On Judgment Day, we think God is going to look at all people, and upon seeing how everyone has fallen short he will say, "Well at least these people aren't as bad as some of the others!" But God doesn't use other people as the standard. He only judges by one standard—his law. God's law leaves no excuses, and it doesn't let you off the hook just because you haven't committed murder or adultery (at least, not physically). Coveting gets to the heart of the issue. It's not something that we typically think of as a big deal. No one sees it, and it's really easy to hide. When Paul saw that coveting was forbidden, he realized that his view of sin was all wrong. Sin is not an issue of external behaviors, but of the heart. And as the prophet Jeremiah tells us, the heart is deceitful and wicked (Jer. 17:9). The law shows us that we are dead in sin.

The Law and Repentance

In his ministry, John the Baptist proclaimed the famous words, "Repent, for the kingdom of heaven is at hand!" This idea of repentance is central to the message of Scripture, and repentance demonstrates the importance of God's law. God uses his law as an instrument to bring us to a state of contrition and repentance.

There are two parts of repentance: contrition, and faith in God's forgiveness. The Holy Spirit uses the law to bring about the first part of repentance. The law brings us to a state of contrition, which is sorrow over sin. Without an understanding of the reality and depth of sin, we will not look for the remedy for sin. The law demonstrates that one has committed evil actions, and has deeply offended God by doing so. Scripture also speaks of a false sorrow over sin, such as that demonstrated by Judas. True repentance, however, is not simply sorrow over the fact that one got caught, but over sin itself.

If one has a conversion experience as an adult (and not everyone does) then they will come to a state of contrition before converting to the Christian faith. Non-Lutheran preachers in the Great Awakening such as John Wesley and George Whitefield proclaimed God's law boldly in this context, and brought many people to saving faith in the gospel. However, for Wesley, and for many Christians today, the law only serves this function *before* one comes to faith. After one's conversion, they are then expected to reach for a type of Christian perfectionism, wherein sin ceases to be a profound problem in the Christian life. This might seem like a nice thought, but it is ultimately untrue. This is demonstrated by both Scripture and Christian experience. For Lutherans, God's law *always* accuses. This is what theologians have called the primary function of the law. While the law does serve other functions, which will be discussed later, this is the most important. Throughout our lives God's law continues to convict us of our shortcomings, because each day is a battle with the sin-nature that resides in each of us.

In the first of his famous 95 Theses, Martin Luther stated that the entire life of the Christian should be one of repentance. God's law is not to be set aside after conversion; we need it daily. It is the continual duty of the believer to judge their lives according to God's law. This can be done by reading through the Ten Commandments each evening, and then thinking about how one lived that particular day in light of God's requirements. The law serves as a mirror, showing us who we truly are. And not only prior to our conversion, but even as Christians, it exposes us as sinners. God does not take away all of our sin at once. Christian growth is a long process, and no matter how long we live, we will never arrive at where we should be. Thus the law continues to accuse us each day of our lives.

God's Solution: The Gospel

The law is not God's final word to us. He did not give us a law to condemn us only to leave us in that state of condemnation. Rather, he gave us the law to diagnose our problem so that we might then search for the remedy. God could not have given us the gospel without the law. Picture a doctor approaching you and telling you that you should take a medicine that he then hands you a prescription for. You have no idea why, and as far as you know, you are perfectly healthy. Most likely, you would not take the medicine (and probably shouldn't!). Now, picture if that same doctor called you and told you that you had a deadly disease, and that he had a cure for it. He then writes you a life-saving prescription. In that first situation, the medicine would not seem like good news at all, because you were not aware of the problem. But in the second scenario, the same news becomes the best news of your life!

The gospel does not bring contrition or sorrow on account of sin. That is the effect of the law. The gospel has its own unique role in God's plan of redemption. The gospel is God's promise. In God's law, we are told what we should do, and in the gospel, we are told what God has done *for* us. These two messages, though not contradictory, are distinct and they must be kept separate, so that one does not look for contrition in the gospel or salvation in the law.

As we looked at how Paul discusses the law in the book of Romans, we can also look at how he speaks about the gospel in his letter. After coming to the conclusion that the law cannot save, but convicts guilty sinners, he expounds upon the righteousness of God which comes "apart from the law" for all those who believe (Rom. 3:21-22). The law shows us that we have no righteousness to offer to God, that we cannot save ourselves by our own strength. The gospel shows us that the righteousness we need to stand before God is not our own, but it is given as a free gift of God's grace.

In short, the gospel is the message of what Jesus Christ has done for the salvation of the world. He was born of a virgin, lived a sinless life, died on the cross, and rose from the grave. The gospel does not contain any commandments or admonitions, but it is a pure promise. The term "gospel" means "good news." News is something that is reported on. It's an event which happened objectively in history that is then explained. A command is, by definition, not news. The gospel is good news; in fact, it's the best news one will ever hear! The gospel is the message that Jesus Christ has won salvation for the world!

In some churches, the gospel is viewed primarily as a message for unbelievers. The message of the forgiveness of sins is proclaimed when people first feel the guilt of their sin, but it gradually loses its importance. The Christian life is described only in terms of moral living, and the gospel gets lost in the mix. This approach misses the importance of God's word of redemption. The gospel is not simply part of the Christian message, but it is the center and driving force of the entire Christian faith. The message of the salvation that Christ has won for sinners is the fuel and sustenance of the Christian life. Just as the law should be heard and contemplated daily, so should the gospel.

The gospel is necessary to understand the second part of repentance. Through the law, the believer experiences contrition, or sorrow for sins. Then, one looks to the gospel for forgiveness and absolution. This is the second, and most important, aspect of repentance. We turn away from our sin, as we see its offense toward God, and turn to Christ who forgives sinners. If repentance is a daily reality, as Luther says, then forgiveness is also a daily reality. There is a sense in which conversion is a daily reality for Christians. This does not mean that we lose our salvation each day and need to become Christians again, but we need to turn away from our sin to the grace of God. This means that as we daily look at our lives through the mirror of God's law, we also daily look to Christ and his promises.

Differences and Similarities between Law and Gospel

The distinction between the law and the gospel is something which is essential for us to grasp in the Christian life. If we neglect the law, then we might be tempted to forget all moral norms, and abuse the gospel. We no longer see the gospel as the *solution* to sin, but as an *excuse* to sin. If we neglect the gospel, on the other hand, then we become legalistic, focusing only on morality and leaving people without hope of salvation. One way in which the law and gospel can be helpfully divided is by looking at their similarities and differences.

There are many ways in which the law and the gospel are similar. First, both have God as their source. God gives both commands and promises. Because the origin of the law and the gospel are from a good and holy God, then both the law and the gospel are good and holy. Second, the law and the gospel both have the same goal—the salvation of sinners. The law was not given so that sinners might be condemned and go to hell. Rather, the law was given so that people might then be ready to hear the gospel. God's goal in the law is to drive people to the gospel, and in the gospel, sinners are saved. Third, both the law and the gospel are taught in both Testaments. We might be tempted to think that the Old Testament is all law, and the New Testament is all gospel. This is not correct, as there are many gracious promises throughout the Old Testament, and God gives many commands in the New Testament.

There are also many differences between the law and the gospel. They differ in their effect upon sinners. Though they both have the goal of salvation, God's commands and his promises play different roles. The law shows people that they are sinners, and leads them to a state of contrition. The gospel shows them what Christ has done for their salvation. They are also different types of speech. The law is a set of commandments, telling people what they are to do. The gospel is news. It is a fact about the salvation won for the world by Christ, and the promises God gives to those who believe. They also differ in their role in Christian living. The law tells the Christian what he should do, but it does not give him the power to do it. The gospel gives the believer the power to begin to obey God's law.

The law and the gospel tell us who we are before God. In the law, we see that we are sinners, and that we have no righteousness of our own. In the gospel, we see that God desires to save us, not by our own righteousness, but by the passive and alien righteousness of Jesus Christ.

Resources for Further Reading:

Dobberstein, Leroy A. *Law and Gospel: Bad News-Good News*. Milwaukee: Northwestern, 1996.

Giertz, Bo. *The Hammer of God*. Minneapolis: Augsburg, 2005.

Luther, Martin. *Galatians*. Crossway Classic Commentaries. Edited by J.I. Packer and Allister McGrath. Wheaton, IL: Crossway, 1998.

Walther, C.F.W. *The Proper Distinction Between Law and Gospel*. Translated by C.H. Dau. Fairfield, IA: Just and Sinner, 2014.

Walther, C.F.W. and Walter C. Pieper. *God's No and God's Yes*. St. Louis: Concordia, 1973.

CHAPTER 4

CHRIST FOR US

In his treatise entitled *Against Latomus*, Martin Luther makes a distinction between two aspects of what Christ does to save us. He writes that Jesus is both the *favor* of God, and a *gift* of God. These two aspects of Jesus' work for us are essential for us to understand if we are going to see how Jesus has both won salvation for us in history, and how we live now as Christians before the world with Christ living in us. In this chapter, we are going to look at what it means that Christ is the favor of God toward us, that salvation is purely an act of divine grace. In the next chapter, we will look at what it means that Christ is now in us.

Understanding Grace

The word "grace" is used often in the church. We like to sing Amazing Grace, and tell people how grace has changed our lives, and that God, in his grace, has done all sorts of things for us. Yet, even though we talk about it constantly in the church, I'm not sure that many of us have a proper understanding of grace. Is grace something that lives within us? Is it some kind of a substance that God gives us in our souls? Or is it the favor of God?

There was a lot of contention around the term "grace" at the time of the Reformation. For many in the Roman Church, grace was viewed as a substance. It was placed into the soul through the sacraments, so that through grace the Christian was changed inwardly. Since Scripture connects grace and salvation (Eph. 2:8), and grace was defined as something which changes the person, then salvation became attributed to a change *within* the Christian. This amounted to a confusion of justification and sanctification, which is why Rome still teaches that justification is a process whereby the believer is changed, rather than a judicial verdict of God upon the sinner.

The reformers contended that the term "grace," in its most proper sense, is the unmerited favor of God. All of those verses that talk about the grace that saves are not then talking about the change which occurs in the believer, but instead they are talking about the way in which God looks upon us. Grace tells us something about God, rather than something about us. Grace tells us that God looks upon us, not with judgment, but with compassion and love. He looks upon us as if we were completely and perfectly righteous, because we are found in Christ rather than within ourselves.

The grace of God is the foundation of our salvation. This grace does not begin simply when we were converted, but God's plan of salvation began before we were even born. Paul writes about this in the first chapter of his epistle to the Ephesians.

Blessed be the God and Father of our Lord Jesus Christ, who has blessed us in Christ with every spiritual blessing in the heavenly places, even as he chose us in him before the foundation of the world, that we should be holy and blameless before him. In love he predestined us for adoption as sons through Jesus Christ, according to the purpose of his will, to the praise of his glorious grace, with which he has blessed us in the Beloved. (Eph. 1:3-6)

This is the doctrine of election. Through this teaching, we see that God's favor toward us precedes our birth. Before you were conceived, before the world itself was created, God predestined you to be adopted as his own child. When foreseeing the mess of sin that the human race was going to be in after the fall, God could have justly decided to reject all of us, and leave us unto his judgment. We would have deserved it. But in an amazing and unexpected way, God looked down upon the sinful world, and instead of rejecting us, he chose us unto salvation!

Note that Paul says we are chosen "through Jesus Christ." If we want to see the grace of God, we only need to look to the person of Jesus Christ. He is the embodiment of the grace of God, and the Father does not give us any favor apart from him. When God chose us to be saved, he also chose the way in which we would be saved—through the death of his Son. And this was a *willing* death on Jesus' part. God the Son was not forced by his Father to do this, but he volunteered his own life, as an act of unmerited love toward his creation.

The Incarnation of Christ

The favor of God is shown all throughout what Jesus has done for sinners, and this begins with the act of the incarnation. At the incarnation, the eternal Son of God condescended to earth and became part of his own creation.

Many of us have seen the television shows where the CEO of some large corporation goes undercover, and becomes part of the lowest paying, most menial job within his company. Through this experience, he learns how valuable these people in the company are, and the hard work that they do which is often forgotten. Christ too came incognito.

Even though he was the world's Creator, most of humanity did not recognize Christ as he walked this earth. The apostle John writes: "He was in the world, and the world was made through him, yet the world did not know him" (John 1:10). God came into the world, and yet the world rejected him.

Christ's life in the world, in which he was rejected by his own creation, is often referred to as his *humiliation*. This word is not being used in the way that we think about it today, such as when you do something really embarrassing. Humiliation, rather, is referring to Jesus' *humility*. Though being God in essence, Jesus humbled himself in a human form, living a humble life, even unto his death on the cross.

Though Christ's incarnation does not save in and of itself, it is an essential aspect of human redemption. Without the incarnation, Jesus could not have died, and he could not have risen from the dead. Through his incarnation, Jesus united God and man into one person in what is known as the *hypostatic union*. Jesus was not just partly man. He took on himself more than simply the appearance of a human body. And He also did not simply take on the *body* of a human, but he has a human body, soul, and will. It was only by becoming a man that Jesus could redeem humanity. If God only assumed *part* of the human constitution, then humanity could not possibly be saved. There is a famous saying from the church fathers which says, "that which was not assumed could not be redeemed."[2] Without the incarnation, the human race would not possess salvation, and because of the incarnation, we can again become like God as we were created to be. The likeness to God which was lost at the fall has been restored through Christ's incarnation. God became man so that man might once again become like God. This

---

[2] This is a paraphrase of: Gregory of Nazianzus. "Epistle 101: Critique of Apollinarius and Apollinarianism," *Early Church Texts*.http://www.earlychurchtexts.com/public/gregoryofnaz_criti que_of_apolliniarianism.htm

does not mean that man literally becomes God (Jesus Christ is the only man who is and will ever be God) but we reflect God's glory, holiness, and righteousness within us as we are redeemed.

Christ's Life under the Law

Jesus was born in a Jewish family, and he lived "under the law" (Gal. 4:4). Like all people, Jesus was obligated to obey God's law. As demonstrated earlier, law-breaking is a universal human problem. God gives us his law as a guide for our lives, so that human creatures know how to please him. But because of sin, we are unable to keep it, and the law now shows us that we need a divine rescuer. If Jesus was going to save us, he would then have to do what we could not. He would have to live a sinless life without breaking any of God's commandments. This is exactly what he did.

God could not have simply forgiven our sins without Christ actually taking care of them. If God is truly just, he can only reward that which is truly righteous and good. Thus God couldn't just *pretend* that we have never sinned, push it out of his mind, and then give us salvation anyway. Instead, for God to save the human race, someone had to earn salvation, and someone also had to pay the penalty of our disobedience. Jesus did both of these things. If Jesus did not have to obey the law for us, then he could have shown up as a grown man at thirty-three, died on the cross, and then rise from the dead. But there is a reason why Jesus came as an infant, and then lived a full life prior to his death. This is often referred to as the *active obedience of Christ*. It is common to speak about Jesus dying in our place, but what we often fail to realize is that Jesus also *lived* in our place. He represented all of us when he was alive on this earth, and he lived a perfect life, so that God would look at Christ's obedience rather than our disobedience. Thus Jesus fulfilled all righteousness for us.

One of the great church fathers, St. Irenaeus, spoke about Jesus' life as a *recapitulation*. In the Garden of Eden, Adam messed up the human race. He lived a sinful life, having disobeyed the divine command to refrain from eating the forbidden fruit. Due to Adam's actions, sin and corruption are part of the human legacy. The human race now has to live with sin, sickness, evil, and death. Throughout his life, Jesus reversed what Adam messed up. He recapitulated the life of Adam, by being put in the same position, but this time doing it correctly. Irenaeus makes the point that Jesus' lived to adulthood so that he could sanctify, or make holy, the entire human life. In Christ, our lives are now holy and the sin of Adam has been reversed.

Christ's Death on the Cross

The most important aspect of Christ's entire work of redemption was his death on the cross. This is at the center of the Christian faith, and should frame the way in which we live our lives as Christians. Paul writes that the entire message of his preaching is "Christ crucified" (1 Cor. 2:2). The Christian life is always lived under the cross.

The centrality of the cross in the Christian faith is rather unique. We have desensitized ourselves to this fact due to our constant use of the cross as a symbol in clothing, art, and design. This has caused us to stop thinking about what the cross actually entails. Stop and think for a minute about what the cross actually is—a Roman torture device. When you wear a cross around your neck, you are displaying one of the most horrific instruments of torture that man has ever invented. Christianity is a bloody religion. The center of our faith is the bloody and painful execution of God. Yet in that death, we have life!

The death of Christ was the death of God. But it was also the death of man. It is on this cross that salvation is won for the world, and that the sins of the whole human race have been paid for. As Christ died, he took all human sin and suffering upon his shoulders, and when he gave up his last breath, all of these evils were defeated.

One model of explaining the cross is as a battle ground. There is a spiritual battle happening in the story of the crucifixion, where Satan thinks that he has trapped Jesus. He attempts to conquer God by inspiring Judas to betray him, and the Roman leaders to kill him. By all human appearances, Jesus had been defeated. In this cosmic battle, however, Jesus turns the evil intentions of the devil around. What the devil thought he had done to defeat Jesus was actually what Jesus had planned from eternity past. This death was ultimately going to be the defeat of Satan. In the death of Christ, Satan strikes the heal of Jesus, but unbeknownst to him, Jesus actually crushes the devil's head (Genesis 3:15).

Scripture also speaks of the death of Jesus as a vicarious death. This means that Jesus' death was accomplished in our place. On the cross, Jesus took the place of sinners. Just as Adam represented the human race prior to the fall, Jesus represents fallen humanity on the cross. This is what is often called the *passive obedience of Christ*. Not only did Jesus *actively* live a life of perfect righteousness on our behalf, but he also passively took the penalty of the law upon himself. All people owe a great debt to God due to our sin, and this debt is death. This was the penalty God imposed upon Adam about in the garden. If Adam ate of the forbidden tree, he would face the penalty of death. We all face this penalty. God cannot be just and set us free without *someone* taking this penalty. Jesus stepped in our place, and took this penalty upon himself.

Picture that you have committed some terrible crime, and you know that your guilt is obvious. You stand before the judge, waiting to hear the sentence. You are absolutely sure that you are going to have to spend your life in prison because that's the penalty you deserve for your crime. Just before the judge is about to render a guilty verdict, an innocent man steps in on your behalf. He says: "Judge, I know that this person is guilty, and I know that I am innocent. Yet, I have compassion for them, and I will serve this life sentence for them, so that they can go free." More accurately, perhaps, it is the *judge himself* who offers to pay for the crime. This is exactly what Jesus does for us! What amazing grace we have!

The Resurrection of Christ

Even though death overtook Jesus, he could not stay in the tomb. Even death itself has no power over God. On the third day, Jesus rose miraculously from the tomb. This begins the period of Christ's life known as the *exaltation*. Christ first humbled himself when coming into the world, and he had to do this in order to take sin upon himself. But after death had been defeated, Christ then takes his place as victor over sin death and the devil. This began immediately after his death, when Jesus descended into hell to proclaim victory over the devils who thought they had defeated him (1 Pet. 3:19), and it continued through his resurrection and ascension.

I often hear Christians refer to the resurrection as proof that the cross actually did what Christ said it would do. Others claim that the resurrection happened to prove Christ's deity. While both of these things are certainly true, they do not grasp the central purpose for the resurrection of Christ. Christ's rising from the dead is not just an afterthought. It's not something that happens after the cross to show what happened through his death, but it is an essential part of redemption itself. Without the resurrection of Christ, there would be no hope for us.

In his first letter to Timothy, Paul cites what many to believe an early Christian hymn, or a part of an early liturgy.

> *He was manifested in the flesh,*
> *vindicated by the Spirit,*
> *seen by angels,*
> *proclaimed among the nations,*
> *believed on in the world,*
> *taken up in glory.* (1 Tim. 3:16)

In this beautiful description of the exaltation of Christ, Paul mentions that Jesus was "vindicated by the Spirit." The term for "vindicated" here is the same term that Paul uses for "justified." It might be more accurate to say that Christ was justified by the Spirit. Why would Paul speak this way? As we saw earlier, justification is something that sinners need so that we might be saved. What does Jesus need to be declared righteous for? Well, like everything else Christ did while he was on this earth, he was justified *for us*. At his resurrection, God declared Jesus to be righteous, not by giving him the righteousness of someone else, but because Jesus actually *is* righteous! The vindication of Jesus at his resurrection is our vindication. His justification is our justification. In him, the entire human race has been justified. The world has been declared righteous, and vindicated before the Father. This is what is called *objective justification*. This justification becomes ours through faith, which is called *subjective justification*. Subjective does not mean, in this context, that it only exists in our mind or our feelings, but refers to the fact that this righteousness is granted to us *personally* and *individually*.

Christ's Intercession

The saving work of Jesus did not end with his resurrection, nor did it end with his ascension. These acts of Christ were all that was necessary for him to *obtain* salvation for the human race, but this salvation needs to be *applied* to us. If we are not united to Christ in faith, then all that Jesus has done for us will remain apart from us. We must repent and believe to receive all of the gifts of God. Christ desires that we would receive all of his blessings, and one of the ways in which he does this is by interceding for us before his heavenly Father. He speaks on our behalf, continually placing his work of redemption before the Father, and thereby assuring that salvation will be given to us.

The reality of who Christ is for us is at the heart of the Christian faith. Without understanding this, any talk about living in the Christian life is meaningless. We must always talk about what Christ has done *for us* as the foundation for what Christ also does *in us*.

Resources for Further Reading:

Gerberding, George Henry. *The Way of Salvation in the Lutheran Church*. American Lutheran Classics Vol. 1. Fairfield, IA: Just and Sinner, 2013, 139-146.

Molstad, John A. *Predestination: Chosen in Christ*. Milwaukee: Northwestern, 1997.

Mueller, Wayne D. *Justification: How God Forgives*. Milwaukee: Northwestern, 2002.

Remensnyder, Junius M. *The Lutheran Manual*. American Lutheran Classics Volume 8. Fairfield, IA: Just and Sinner, 2014, 27-32.

Sartorius, Ernst. *The Doctrine of the Person and Work of Christ*. Fairfield, IA: Just and Sinner, 2014.

Voigt, A.G. *Biblical Dogmatics*. American Lutheran Classics Volume 3. Fairfield, IA: Just and Sinner, 2013, 137-164.

CHAPTER 5

CHRIST IN US

In the last chapter, we talked about the essential theme of "Christ for us," and that the only hope any sinner has for salvation is through the objective work of Christ. This is what Martin Luther described as the *favor* of God. Along with these essential truths, Scripture also speaks about another important aspect of the Christian faith—Christ *in us*. This is what Luther called the *gift* of God. Jesus is the favor of God, insofar as he wins salvation outside of us, and he is the gift of God insofar as he is given to us and dwells within us.

Before discussing the reality of Christ within us, some important points must be made regarding the distinction between these two truths. Andreas Osiander, an early follower of Martin Luther, argued that believers are justified because the divine nature indwells them. This position was rejected by the Lutheran church, because it was a confusion of these two categories. If we look for justification in something that Christ is doing within us, then we look for assurance in our own hearts. This takes our eyes off of what Jesus did for us in history. This can cause us to lose our assurance, and to downplay the importance of Christ's death. On the other hand, when we neglect to speak about Christ in us, and focus only on the favor of God, we miss an essential aspect of what it means to be a Christian. We might be tempted to think that how God is changing us does not matter, or that the way in which we live is irrelevant.

A helpful way to distinguish these two categories of Christ as favor and Christ as gift is to think about the distinction between the two kinds of righteousness. Passive righteousness, or our justification, is concerned with Christ as the favor of God, or what Christ has done for us outside of us. Thus, when we are speaking about ourselves *coram Deo* (before God), we must emphasize what Christ has done *for* us. However, when we are speaking about our relationships in this world, our perspective changes. As we live out our daily lives, and think about how we should treat others and what decisions we should make during the day, our focus should be on Christ *in us*. Jesus, as a gift that is given to us in faith, helps us to walk in God's will, and uses us to bless and serve others. Active righteousness, or our righteousness *coram mundo* (before the world), is all about what Christ is doing *in* us; passive righteousness, or our righteousness *coram Deo*, is all about what Christ has done *for* us.

Sanctification: Broad and Narrow

One of the terms that Scripture uses to describe the change that God works within us as Christians is *sanctification*. This has also been called *renovation* and *new obedience*. The term "sanctification" is used in two divergent ways in Scripture. In the broad sense, as it has been called by Lutheran theologians, sanctification refers to all that God does for the believer in Christ. This is what Paul means when he says: "you are in Christ Jesus, who became to us wisdom from God, righteousness and sanctification and redemption" (1 Cor. 1:30). Jesus is our sanctification, and we are completely and perfectly sanctified if we are in him. In this sense, sanctification is a perfect state that we live in because of what Christ has done.

On the other hand, sanctification can be used in a *narrow* sense. In this way of speaking, sanctification refers to the process of Christian growth that happens within us. When speaking about this sense, we are not talking about something that is perfect. Our Christian growth is always very far from where it should be. But there is a progressive work that happens within us, wherein God makes us more like himself.

The word "sanctify" simply means "to make holy." Holiness refers to the distinctness of who God is in opposition to creation, and especially to sinful creation. To be holy is to be "set apart." In the broad sense then, sanctification refers to the fact that we are completely and perfectly holy before God (*coram Deo*) because of what Jesus Christ has done for us. There is nothing we can possibly do to add to that finished work of Jesus. We are only holy because *he* is holy, and we are in him. In the narrow sense, sanctification is the fact that we are in the process of being *made* holy. This is where, before the world (*coram mundo*), we are gradually becoming more like Christ, as we turn away from sin, and God helps us to live according to his will.

Regeneration: the New Life we have in Christ

If we are going to be made holy, something radical has to happen to us. Scripture tells us that we are conceived in iniquity (Psalm 51:5), that we are dead in trespasses and sins (Eph. 2:1), that we are at enmity with God (Rom. 8:7), and that we do not seek God (Rom. 3:11). We are anything but holy when we are born. This is apparent when observing the actions of in infant. They will do absolutely anything to get what they want. If they possessed the strength to do so, an infant would rip their own parent's arms off to get what they desire. We are all born curved in on ourselves, looking only at our own needs and wants, rather than those of others. We are enslaved to the devil. In and of ourselves, we will never become holy.

God does a miraculous work within us. He takes us—who don't want anything to do with him—and causes us to love him. He grants us faith as a free gift. We usually think of faith as some kind of human decision. We like to think that our own determination and will-power can create faith in our hearts. But, if we are truly dead in our sins, as Scripture tells us, then how can we possibly free ourselves from this dilemma? How can we be made alive? If you were to walk into a graveyard, could you convince a dead body to wake themselves up? What if you were really convincing, and had all the right words to say? Of course not! Corpses cannot bring themselves to life, and in the same way, spiritually dead people cannot bring life to themselves.

In his letter to Titus, Paul speaks about this act of God as "the washing of regeneration" (Tit. 3:5). Through the washing which occurs in Holy Baptism, Christians experience a *regeneration*, or a re-creation. Something radical happens. Our old self is suddenly destroyed, which previously hated God and had no spiritual impulses, and God raises us up as new creatures who love God and who want to serve him. This is often described as being "born again." This is how Jesus speaks to Nicodemus in John 6. Upon Nicodemus asking his ministry and identity, Jesus says:

"Truly, truly, I say to you, unless one is born again he cannot see the kingdom of God." Nicodemus said to him, "How can a man be born when he is old? Can he enter a second time into his mother's womb and be born?" Jesus answered, "Truly, truly, I say to you, unless one is born of water and the Spirit, he cannot enter the kingdom of God. That which is born of the flesh is flesh, and that which is born of the Spirit is spirit. (John 3:3-6)

Our rebirth is a result of the Holy Spirit. We are born as flesh, as sinful people, and we must be born anew if we are to have any spiritual life within us. Jesus tells Nicodemus that one is born again through two things: water and Spirit. In Baptism, God has united his Spirit to water, and as we receive the name of the Father, Son, and Holy Spirit upon us, we are born again! It is only by being born again that a new spiritual life can begin in us.

Living the Sanctified Life
All people who have faith will also have good works. The same faith which receives the forgiveness of sins also does works of love and service for other people. There are two aspects to faith: First, it is receptive, and second it is operative. Before God, faith simply receives salvation. Before the world, however, this same faith is active. It demonstrates itself through good deeds. Sometimes these works can just be performed spontaneously by the Spirit, without us even thinking about it. When people first convert to the Christian faith, they get extremely excited about their newfound salvation in Christ, and they are so excited that they can't wait to get to church. They often want to read their Bible every day, and spend a lot of time in prayer. They go around telling all of their friends about Jesus. These works are never compulsory. Instead, they just want to do it!

It would be a great blessing if that same kind of excitement of the new convert would stay with us throughout our Christian lives, but things do change. Anyone who has been in a relationship for a long time knows this. At the beginning of a new relationship, kindness is easy. When those feelings first appear toward another person, your words flow easily, and you find yourself interested in absolutely everything that the other person has to say. But after some time, that relationship begins to change. After being married for a number of years, the relationship that spouses have with one another grows and evolves. The couple becomes more accustomed to one another, and acts of love and kindness are no longer spontaneous. That initial chemistry that someone feels toward a spouse is not the same. Now one has to be intentional about time with the other partner. You have to make a conscious effort to continue to work for the good of the other person. Our relationship with God works in the same way. There are times when that relationship might get stale. We don't feel the same kind of excitement that we used to about God, and so it is not as natural for us to read Scripture or pray regularly, and we don't try and bring Jesus up to our unbelieving friends. God's love for us is unchanging, but our love for God is ever-shifting due to our sinful and selfish existence.

The sanctified life takes effort. God calls us to try and do the things which please him. We do have to consciously spend time in God's Word, in prayer, and doing what God wants us to do. Paul tells this to the Thessalonians, writing:

Finally, then, brothers, we ask and urge you in the Lord Jesus, that as you received from us how you ought to walk and to please God, just as you are doing, that you do so more and more. For you know what instructions we gave you through the Lord Jesus. For this is the will of God, your sanctification: that you abstain from sexual immorality; that each one of you know how to control his own body in holiness and honor, not in the passion of lust like the Gentiles who do not know God; that no one transgress and wrong his brother in this matter, because the Lord is an avenger in all these things, as we told you beforehand and solemnly warned you. For God has not called us for impurity, but in holiness. Therefore whoever disregards this, disregards not man but God, who gives his Holy Spirit to you. (1 Thess. 4:1-8)

Paul urges the Thessalonians unto their sanctification, which he identifies as the will of God that is connected to specific commandments. His words are pretty harsh where at the end Paul writes: "Whoever disregards this, disregards not man but God, who gives his Holy Spirit to you." If we neglect holy living, then we are disregarding God himself! God gave us his Holy Spirit to aid and guide us in this life, that we might follow his will.

While justification and regeneration are purely passive works, where we have absolutely no part, our sanctification is a cooperative effort. We are called to work at it. We must, however, be careful here when talking about our cooperation with God. God does not redeem us through justification at the beginning of the Christian life, and then just leave us on our own. He doesn't leave the work of Christian living solely up to us. The only reason why we can cooperate at all with God's grace, is because God has made us his own children, and has given us new spiritual life. Apart from God's work, we would never do any good work. It's also important to note that this is not a 50/50 kind of a thing, where God does his half, and then we have to do the other. Instead, it is God who is working behind every good thing that I do, and so when these good works happen, I can't take the credit. Instead, I must give the glory solely to God who has given himself to me.

The Mystical Union

God does not just work on us from the outside, but through faith, he has actually taken a home within our hearts. We serve as a temple, where the holy presence of God dwells. He lives in us, and by doing so, he causes us to be more like himself. This is what theologians have often referred to as the "mystical union." There is some mysterious way in which God himself lives in us, and we are united with him. His own being permeates our being, and his life is lived through us.

When utilizing the term "mystical" we must be careful to explain what we mean. There are certain Christian (and many non-Christian) traditions which speak about mysticism. This can refer to a type of religion which is based on mystical experiences through visions, or meditation. The problem with these approaches to religion is that they focus on one's experience of God apart from Word and Sacrament. We can't find any hope or certainty in our own experiences, but only in the means of grace, where God has promised that we will find it. Oftentimes, when people look for God in their own minds, thoughts, dreams, or whatever else it might be, they come to all sorts of conclusions about the faith which are not consistent with Scripture, but only with their own emotions. Thus, we must be careful when speaking about the mystical union, not to look for God in inward experience, but in the objective means of grace.

Jesus speaks of this mystical union especially in John's gospel where he says: "I am in my Father, and you in me, and I in you" (John 14:20). There is a beautiful mysterious union that the Christian has with Jesus that echoes the union that God the Father has with God the Son. We live in Christ just as he also lives in us. Jesus explains this in terms of the relationship between a vine and its branches: "I am the vine; you are the branches. Whoever abides in me and I in him, he it is that bears much fruit, for apart from me you can do nothing" (John 15:5). Just as the branch of the vine can bear no fruit without being connected to the vine, a Christian can do nothing good without being solidly connected to Christ. There are two aspects to this. First, we are in Christ. We are connected to him and all of the benefits of salvation. Second, Christ is in us, and through his presence within us, we are transformed, and we can live in a way that pleases God.

Paul also discusses this mystical union throughout his letters. There is an instance in his first letter to the Corinthians where Paul responds to all kinds of sexual immorality that were prevalent in the church, and he rebukes them by pointing to this mystical union. He brings up the nature of the sexual union, noting that in this intimate act "two become one flesh" (1 Cor. 6:16). If one is engaging in these acts with a prostitute, then they are becoming "one flesh" with a prostitute. This sin is especially evil, according to Paul, because it disrupts one's union with God. Paul writes that "he who is joined to the Lord becomes one spirit with him" (1 Cor. 6:17), and that the Christian's body is the temple of the Holy Spirit. How disgraceful is it that someone would desecrate the temple of God by uniting it with a prostitute! Paul finishes this section of his letter by encouraging the Corinthians to "Glorify God in your body" (1 Cor. 6:20).

This mystical union should encourage us to refrain from sin in our bodies. It also gives worth to our bodies. When you might suffer from issues of your body image, or be tempted to do something to harm yourself, remember—your body is the temple of the Holy Spirit. That is a significant truth. God himself dwells within you, and you are united with him in your body. This is also a great comfort to those who are experiencing great sorrow. There are times when we all feel like God is very far from us. We feel like he is not actually listening to our prayers, and that maybe something is wrong with our faith. When this happens, remember this truth—God is living in you. He is not far from you, and he is at work within you, even when you can't see it.

It is this union with Christ that is the grounds by which we grow in our sanctification. Paul confesses that, "It is no longer I who live, but Christ lives in me" (Gal. 2:20). The life of good works that we live is not something we can claim as our own, but it is Christ himself living in and through us! As we grow spiritually, Paul tells us that Christ will be "formed in you" (Gal. 4:19). This helps us to avoid any moralistic views of the Christian life, where the emphasis is solely on the believer and his own effort in overcoming sin. Rather, the Christian life is about Christ living in us, for the good of our neighbor. And he does this by mystically uniting us to himself and dwelling within our hearts.

Resources for Further Reading:

Cooper, Jordan. *Christification: A Lutheran Approach to Theosis.* Eugene, OR: Wipf & Stock, 2014.

Jacobs, Henry Eyster. *A Summary of the Christian Faith.* American Lutheran Classics Volume 6 Part I. Fairfield, IA: Just and Sinner, 2014, 273-312.

Jacobs, Henry Eyster. *Elements of Religion.* American Lutheran Classics Volume 5. Fairfield, IA: Just and Sinner, 2013, 199-209.

Lange, Lyle W. *Sanctification: Alive in Christ.* Milwaukee: Northwestern, 1999.

Senkbeil, Harold L. *Dying to Live: The Power of Forgiveness.* St. Louis: Concordia, 1994.

CHAPTER 6

A CITIZEN OF TWO KINGDOMS

It is said that there are two things that are not good conversation topics in polite company: religion and politics. In this chapter, we are going to discuss both. The topic of politics tends to bring up an immense amount of passion and emotion in people. It's an unfortunate truth that sometimes even Christians identify themselves more-so with their own political party than with Christ himself. This is apparent with the passion some demonstrate in defense of the political views as compared to the passion they demonstrate regarding things of the faith. America, in particular, is a divided nation politically, and because of that, churches have had to answer the question—how do we deal with politics? Some have decided to just avoid politics altogether, and leave that to other venues, whereas others have decided to align themselves with a particular political party. This is made even more difficult by the fact that people claim that there is a large separation between church and state in the fabric of American society itself. So how do we as Christians answer these questions? Is there an answer at all?

Two Realms

We cannot ignore the fact that we live in a culture with a particular government that rules over us. It's a fact, and we can't simply run from culture or ignore the state. We have to deal with the facts of when and where we live. God has placed us, not only in the church, but also in whatever culture and nation we are in. And while problems exist in every culture, and all nations have some level of corruption, it is still a *good* realm in which you, as God's child, are called to live.

Martin Luther talked about the church and the state as two different estates in which all people live. The church is primarily connected with the "right hand kingdom" (the kingdom of grace and forgiveness), and thus has its own particular role and duties tied to it. On the other hand, the broader culture, is tied to the "left hand kingdom," (the kingdom of law and order), and it also has a role to play in God's world, and thus has its own sphere of authority. We shouldn't think only of government when speaking about the left-hand kingdom, because there are many aspects of our lives which are governed by law rather than grace and forgiveness. Some areas of our lives are "secular," meaning that they are not particularly Christian, and you have to function there with both believer and unbeliever.

The distinction between law and gospel, as well as the distinction between active and passive righteousness are helpful here. In the left hand kingdom, everything functions according to the law rather than the gospel. If you get arrested, you can't say to the judge: "But I have the forgiveness of sins!" and expect him to let you off. The gospel, or passive righteousness, does not control or rule the state. If the state worked on the principle of love and forgiveness, then justice would never be served, and the world would be in chaos. Here, the law reigns supreme. In the church, things function rather differently. If the same criminal who was arrested came to the pastor and confessed his sin, the pastor would have a duty, not to punish him, but to absolve his sins. Here, the gospel, and the forgiveness of sins have the final say.

These two ways in which the realms are ruled are not contradictory to one another. One might assume that God rules the church, but he does not rule the state. This, however, would be a misunderstanding. God rules both kingdoms, and he is at work in both kingdoms. He simply works for different ends in each realm. One might ask if God rules both kingdoms, then why doesn't the principle "love your neighbor as yourself" function in the state? Some argue that Jesus' statements about love and the forgiveness of sins mean that we should not go to war, and that our domestic and foreign policies should be based on the Golden Rule or the Beatitudes. Understanding the difference between these two realms helps us to see why this is not a contradiction. God created the state so that there might be some semblance of order in society. And the keeping of order does sometimes mean war, and the punishment of criminals.

Here is an illustration which will help to show how this works. There is a police officer who catches someone who is driving drunk. The police officer pulls him over, and the man who was driving starts to get extremely hostile, and tries to fight arrest. Eventually, this man pulls out a gun and the police officer shoots him to protect himself. Clearly, at this point, the police officer has been working within the left hand kingdom. For the sake of good order, and the protection of his own life, he was perfectly justified in shooting the drunk driver. Thankfully, the drunk driver does not die, but recovers in the local hospital. This same police officer, who shot him, then goes to visit this man in the hospital. He sits next to the man's bedside and talks to him about the forgiveness of sins, and the freedom that he would have in Christ through faith. The officer does not drop the charges against this man, according to the left hand realm, but wants him to receive forgiveness for what he had done in the right hand realm. This shows one individual who is on this cross-section of two totally different kingdoms, with different rules of conduct. We all stand on these cross-roads.

The Institution of Government

God did not create government prior to the fall. There was an order to things, however, as God ruled over Adam, and Adam was the head of his wife. Both Adam and Eve then ruled over the rest of the earth. There was no need, however, for governmental structures without sin. If there was no sin in the world, no crimes would need to be punished, and everyone would play their own part in society freely under God as Lord.

When sin came into the world, things changed. Because sin and evil exist, restraint is necessary, in order to curb evil actions in this world. That such restraint is necessary is apparent from the earliest days of the human race. Murder enters the world in Genesis 4. In this text, Cain is jealous of his brother Able, because Able brought a worthy offering to God, and in anger he slayed him. What is particularly interesting here is that God does not then kill Cain. Instead, he decides that he is going to protect Cain. God put a mark on Cain's head, so that anyone who killed Cain would himself be punished (Gen. 4:15). This is the beginning of the institution of government, where an outwardly evil action has specific consequences must be carried out. The institution of government was essentially founded upon the death penalty.

The necessity of government is demonstrated throughout Scripture. After the flood in the time of Noah, God immediately established, once again, a system of punishment for people who harm one another. He told Noah, "Whoever sheds the blood of man, by man shall his blood be shed" (Gen. 9:6). Throughout the history of the world, governments have always been necessary to protect life, and to assure that a society can function. To live in a system of anarchy is to let sin reign supreme.

God established a particular government in the nation of Israel. In this nation, there was no strict distinction between church and state. The laws God gave them were tied to correct worship and doctrine, as well as morality. Because of this, there are some Christians who argue that church and state should not be separated at all. Some even propose that the laws which governed Israel should govern society today. But we must understand the particular purpose of Israel in the history of redemption. Israel was a unique nation, chosen specifically by God to be that nation in which he would bring forth the Savior of the world. After Christ had accomplished salvation, God's unique workings with Israel ceased. There is no nation today on earth that carries the unique role that Israel had on the earth. Thus, we cannot simply apply the principles given to Israel to the state today.

Two Mandates

There are two specific mandates given to humanity that people are called to live by. Understanding these two very distinct mandates shows us what the difference is between the church and the culture. The first is from the creation of man, which we looked at earlier, where God tells Adam that he is to take care of the Garden, bear children, and watch over the animals. Essentially, Adam must work within creation, and establish human society through producing children. This same mandate is repeated after the flood. God said to Noah and his sons:

Be fruitful and multiply and fill the earth. The fear of you and the dread of you shall be upon every beast of the earth and upon every bird of the heavens, upon everything that creeps on the ground and all the fish of the sea. Into your hand they are delivered. (Gen. 9:1-2)

Again, humanity is told that they are required to take care of the earth, rule over the animals, and have children. This is also the context in which God commands that the death penalty be enacted as a punishment for murder. Note that this mandate says nothing about forgiveness, nothing about faith, and nothing about Sacraments. That is because this mandate was given to all people alike. It's the mandate that all humans are to follow. It is about culture and creation. This is why the covenant God establishes with Noah is a creational one. He promises that he would not destroy the *earth* with a flood.

There is another mandate given which has very different rules. This is the Great Commission of Matthew 28.

All authority in heaven and on earth has been given to me. Go therefore and make disciples of all nations, baptizing them in the name of the Father and of the Son and of the Holy Spirit, teaching them to observe all that I have commanded you. And behold, I am with you always, to the end of the age. (Matt. 28:18-20)

This mandate says absolutely nothing about changing the culture, or about punishing criminals. Instead, this mandate is all about the gospel. Jesus commands that his church would baptize in the Triune name, teach the words of Jesus, and evangelize.

We live in the middle of both of these mandates. The Great Commission does not negate the cultural mandate that was given to Adam and to Noah. On the one hand, we are all called to live as part of our culture. We are called to promote the well-being of others and justice in society. On the other, we are called to be a part of God's church, to be baptized, and to bring the gospel to others. Thus, as God's people, we must strive to live rightly in *both* of God's kingdoms, according to how he has structured them.

Christians and Politics
This leads us to the practical question of how we, as Christians are to relate to politics. Having explained the difference between the two realms in which we all live, we can now look at some of the popular proposals from

Christians who have tried to answer this question. In doing so, we will see how someone should faithfully live as a citizen of the left-hand kingdom.

At the time of the Reformation, there were several different religious groups which had grown to prominence. On the one hand there were the *magisterial reformers*, which included the Lutherans, Calvinists, and Anglicans. These groups sought to work within the existing political structures to establish reform in the church. They did not believe that Christians needed to overthrow secular government. On the other hand, there were the Anabaptists. The Anabaptists were a broad group who held to many different theological views. They were united primarily in their rejection of infant baptism. But, despite their differences, the Anabaptists tended to reject traditional approaches to the state. In some circumstances, they argued that true Christians needed to form their own government and overthrow existing power structures. Others argued that Christians should simply ignore politics altogether. This is the approach of modern Anabaptist groups such as the Amish and Mennonites. They argue that one should not vote or serve in political offices, because Christians live in a different kingdom. These groups will often discard traditional ways of dressing seeking to avoid the evil culture of the world. In view of the two kingdoms, the problem with this approach becomes clear. They have rightly emphasized the importance of the right hand kingdom, but have wrongly concluded that the Christian's existence in the church negates their role in the culture.

There are other Christian groups who are extremely active in politics. Sometimes, churches will endorse particular candidates from the pulpit. There is a movement known as Theonomy which argues that the Old Testament civil laws given to Israel need to be adopted by society today. It is the role of the church to fight for the government to establish policies that are in accord with Scripture. These groups rightly teach that Christians should be active in the left hand realm, but wrongly confuse the purpose of the church and the state, by causing the church to emphasize politics rather than the forgiveness of sins, as well as by confusing the role of Israel and that of the modern state.

How Should Christians Vote?

This is an important question, because it affects how we live in society. We are all inundated with phone calls, television programs, and commercials when elections are close, and sometimes we might not be able to make any decisions regarding who we should vote for. So, we ask—who *should* we vote for? Is there a certain political party that is better than another? Which issues are the most essential to Christians?

The Bible does not give us a particular political system to follow. Israel was run as a monarchy, and democracy as we know it today was unknown in the ancient world. All political structures are imperfect, because government itself is the result of the fall. Every state is going to have sinful people running it, and everything sinful people engage is going to be corrupt. No matter how we try to emphasize checks and balances in the state, some people are going to abuse their political power. We should not then look for some kind of perfect political system, because all of them are going to have their flaws, but we should support the one which we think best promotes justice and the good of others.

Even though Scripture does not give explicit statements about economics or the nature of decision making in the government, there are some issues on which Scripture is clear. The modern practice of abortion, for example, is clearly an instance of immorality, as innocent lives are murdered. We know from Scripture that murder is sinful (Ex. 20:13), and that a fetus is a life (Psalm 139:13). Since the role of government is to protect life rather than to take it, Christians should stand united around this issue. Some churches observe one Sunday a year wherein this issue is addressed from the pulpit. This is not a confusion of the two realms, because though distinct, these realms do and should interact with one another. At times, the church must speak with a unified prophetic voice against the immorality of the state. This is what many Christians did during the rise of Hitler, for example.

There is valid room for disagreement among Christians on political issues that are not addressed directly in Scripture. There are three principles which should guide us in making those decisions. First, are there Scriptural principles which might help us take one side of a particular issue? Many people who are fiscally conservative, for example, will argue that their policies are consistent with the Biblical principle that wages should only be given for honest work (2 Thess. 3:10). Those who promote a larger amount of government spending on social programs will argue, on the other hand, that they are being consistent with the Biblical emphasis on caring for the poor (the book of Amos for example). Second, one's decisions should reflect what would be good for the welfare and general order of society. If one feels that a particular policy would promote justice and peace, then they should vote for it. If it does not, they should reject it. Finally, the love of our neighbors should guide our political decisions. We must not think only how laws will affect us, but how they will impact those around us. Within these parameters, Christians can have genuine disagreement.

Respect Owed to Rulers

People in the United States generally do not have a high respect for those in authority over them. As an American, this is built in my DNA. This nation was founded by people who were fighting against a tyrannical government, and thus there has always been skepticism of authority within the American culture.

There will be many leaders of whatever nation we live in who we do not like. There will be leaders who we only want to speak negatively about. While we are tempted to treat leaders with contempt, God urges us to show reverence for the leaders of our world. Paul writes about this in Romans 13:

Let every person be subject to the governing authorities. For there is no authority except from God, and those that exist have been instituted by God. Therefore whoever resists the authorities resists what God has appointed, and those who resist will incur judgment. For rulers are not a terror to good conduct, but to bad. Would you have no fear of the one who is in authority? Then do what is good, and you will receive his approval, for he is God's servant for your good. But if you do wrong, be afraid, for he does not bear the sword in vain. For he is the servant of God, an avenger who carries out God's wrath on the wrongdoer. Therefore one must be in subjection, not only to avoid God's wrath but also for the sake of conscience. For because of this you also pay taxes, for the authorities are ministers of God, attending to this very thing. Pay to all what is owed to them: taxes to whom taxes are owed, revenue to whom revenue is owed, respect to whom respect is owed, honor to whom honor is owed. (Rom. 13:1-7)

What is particularly interesting in this text is that Paul was speaking about an unjust government. The emperor of Rome, when Paul wrote, was Nero. Eventually, Nero would be the first emperor to persecute Christians, including Paul himself. Yet even this unjust ruler is called "the servant of God." Even an evil ruler can be used by God to punish evil and to keep order in society. Thus, we are to treat leaders with respect and honor, even if we don't feel that they deserve it.

Resources for Further Reading:

Deutschlander, Daniel M. *Civil Government: God's Other Kingdom.* Milwaukee: Northwestern, 1998.

Hecht, Bill. *Two Wars We Must Not Lose: What Christians Need to Know About Radical Islamists, Radical Secularists, and Why We Can't Leave the Battle Up to Our Divided Government.* Fort Wayne: Concordia Seminary, 2012.

Heiser, James D. and Jerald Dulas. *The One True God, the Two Kingdoms, and the Three Estates.* Malone, TX: Repristination, 2011.

Menuge, Angus L. (Editor). *Christ and Culture in Dialogue: Constructive Themes and Practical Applications.* St. Louis: Concordia, 1999.

Wright, William J. Martin *Luther's Understanding of God's Two Kingdoms: A Response to the Challenge of Skepticism.* Grand Rapids: Baker, 2010.

CHAPTER 7

THE IMITATION OF CHRIST

We all have people in our lives who we look at up to as examples of virtue. Those of us who are parents have a duty to be models to our children, because it is inevitable that they will imitate the way that we live. There are other great examples of love and self-sacrifice, who have gotten extensive recognition for the way in which they lived. We will not model a righteous life if we do not see people who are living a righteous life. There was an old practice, which is unfortunately no longer common, of young people having mentors. These mentors would show them how to live, how to handle certain situations, and most importantly, how to grow spiritually. We can think of Martin Luther's relationship with his spiritual father Johann Staupitz. Throughout his times of intense spiritual struggle, Luther turned to Staupitz, who continued to comfort him by reminding him of the love of Christ. The words and actions of Staupitz had an immense influence upon Luther's own life, thought, and character. It is good for all of us to find someone who we look up to in these ways. I recommend finding two spiritual mentors: one who is alive, and one who is dead. There is a lot of wisdom that can be gained from great spiritual figures in the past, and we would do well to adopt one of them as our own, and read their books throughout our lives. It is also good to find someone who is alive today, who can guide you in specific ways throughout your life, giving you spiritual guidance and a Christian example.

There are many good spiritual examples throughout Scripture, both in the Old and the New Testament. We can look at the great faith of Noah, who believed God's Word that a flood was coming, and spent years building an ark. Or we can look at David, who despite his great sin always looked to God for help, and when confronted with his sin, immediately repented and changed his ways. We can look at the life of the Apostle Paul, who lived his entire life for the sake of Christ, even to the point of dying for his confession of faith. But all of these figures, no matter how faithful and holy, were still sinners. Even the greatest saints in Scripture demonstrate that they too are sinners.

Christ as our Example

There is no better example of holy living than Christ himself. He is the only man who ever lived a sinless and perfect life, and so when we are attempting to live lives of virtue, of following God's will, we should look to Christ himself. Some traditions have argued that Jesus' work on this earth was primarily to give us a good example of how to live. They argue that the cross is not a substitutionary sacrifice on behalf of humanity, but instead, it is a selfless act performed by a man which then gives us an example of how to live selfless lives. This approach is deeply flawed. When speaking about the imitation of Christ, we must always remember that we only imitate Christ in view of his work as Savior. Redemption always primary, and Christ's work as exemplar is secondary, though not unimportant.

When we speak of Christ as our example, we must be careful not to assume that we need to repeat every action that Jesus took. Jesus did a lot of things which we, as God's people, are not necessarily called to do. For example, Christ performed all sorts of miracles. He raised the dead. That does not mean that we have the same authority as Christ to do the same. God does not promise us the ability to give sight to the blind, hearing to the deaf, and life to the dead. We are also not all called to die a life of martyrdom. Jesus cleansed the temple with a whip. That doesn't mean that we are called to go into our local mega-church that has a book store and start turning bookshelves over. These are aspects of Jesus' life which were a unique part of his calling as the Son of God and messiah.

Imitating Christ's Humility

So if there is any encouragement in Christ, any comfort from love, any participation in the Spirit, any affection and sympathy, complete my joy by being of the same mind, having the same love, being in full accord and of one mind. Do nothing from selfish ambition or conceit, but in humility count others more significant than yourselves. Let each of you look not only to his own interests, but also to the interests of others. Have this mind among yourselves, which is yours in Christ Jesus, who, though he was in the form of God, did not count equality with God a thing to be grasped, but emptied himself, by taking the form of a servant, being born in the likeness of men. And being found in human form, he humbled himself by becoming obedient to the point of death, even death on a cross. Therefore God has highly exalted him and bestowed on him the name that is above every name, so that at the name of Jesus every knee should bow, in heaven and on earth and under the earth, and every tongue confess that Jesus Christ is Lord, to the glory of God the Father. (Phil. 2:1-11)

Acting in humility is one of the hardest things for us sinful people to do. Sin, in essence, is caring more about ourselves than about others. We are born curved in on our own wants and desires. I mentioned earlier the nature of infants, who cry continually until they get what they want. As we age, this self-obsession remains. When toddlers are in the toy store, and they find something that they really want, they will demand it from their parents. And when they are told "no," they often will throw a temper tantrum, scream, cry, and whatever else gets them attention, simply because they didn't get what they wanted. When we get older, we like to think that we've outgrown these childish ways. In reality, we don't get less selfish as we get older; we simply find better ways of getting what we want. Instead of demanding things from others, we find ways to manipulate people into having our desires fulfilled. When we start working, and earning our own money, we don't have to demand that others buy us things we desire. Instead, we can do it quietly by using our money on ourselves rather than others.

Humility is not valued by contemporary culture. Think about those who are the role models in our culture: movie stars, musicians, and others who have fame and money. Our culture is obsessed with celebrity. As you walk through the aisles at the local grocery store, you will see many magazines with stories about celebrities, talking about the third or fourth marriage of some famous actress. These are people with money, power, and pride. If you listen to popular rap music, you know that rappers tend to brag about their own talent and achievements. We are encouraged to speak highly of ourselves, to think only about our own wants and desires rather than those of others.

When Paul speaks about humility, he talks about Christ. No one is a greater example of humility than Jesus Christ himself. Jesus, though being in essence God, became a man. And as a man, he lived a humble life. He didn't demonstrate his power. He did not even speak to others about who he was until he

began his ministry at thirty years old. This humility
shows itself most powerfully in his death. Jesus did not
speak back to others when he was attacked, but he
allowed the Roman government to take his own life.

We should be humble because Jesus was
humble. This is a great example of how it is the gospel
which motivates sanctified living. As we hold the
gospel before us, looking at the life of Jesus Christ, and
what he has done for us, we will be filled with such
great joy because of the salvation that Jesus has won for
us. We will gain a desire to live the same way before
others. While we cannot save others in the way that
Jesus saved us by his humility, we can still live a life of
blessing to others, by considering their needs before our
own. When doing this, we become "little Christs" to
others, as Christ lives his own life in and through us.

Love one Another

*A new commandment I give to you, that you love one
another: just as I have loved you, you also are to love one
another. By this all people will know that you are my
disciples, if you have love for one another.* (John 13:34-35)

Love is the essence of Jesus' life. As the Apostle John
tells us, God *is* love (1 John 4:8). Everything that Jesus
did in his life was out of his pure unmerited love. It was
love by which God predestined you unto salvation. It
was by love that Jesus was sent into the world in human
flesh. It was by love that Jesus gave up his own life on

the cross. It was by love that God sent his Holy Spirit to you, to change your heart, grant you faith in Christ, and promise you eternal life. None of this is deserved, but God loves freely.

Because love is the essence of God, love is also the essence of his commandments. Remember that God's commandments reflect his own nature and character. Jesus summarizes God's commandments with two simple ideas: love God and love your neighbor (Matt. 22:37-29). These two different parts of the law are often called the "two tables" of the law. The first three commandments are directed toward God and our worship to him. The final seven commandments refer to the manner in which we are called to love those around us. As we strive to obey God's commandments, we strive to love God and one another.

We have to define exactly what love is when speaking about the importance of this commandment. In our culture, people talk a lot about love, but we have redefined what love means. When people use the phrase "God is love," what they often really mean is "love is God." They define God as *only* love, and then define love by whatever they think it means and import that meaning on the text of Scripture. People often define love in such a way as to negate any judgment whatsoever. To love is to ignore sin and not to speak out about any behavior that is opposed to God's Word. When pastors call out sin as sin we are told, "but God is love. You cannot judge." We can't define God by our concept of love, but we must define love according to who God is.

Jesus models the love that we are called to have with one another in his own life. When looking at Jesus' life, we see that love does not mean that we do not judge sin. Think about Jesus' continual stern words to the Pharisees. He calls them a brood of vipers (Matt. 23:33), children of the devil (John 8:44), and hypocrites (Matt. 23:28). He also was quite harsh when he drove the money changers out of the temple (Matt. 21:12). He also affirmed the entirety of the Old Testament, which includes the clear statements about man's sin and God's wrath against sin (Matt. 5:17). To love then, is not to ignore sin, or to deny the reality of God's wrath. Jesus took sin very seriously. He took it so seriously that he gave his own life for it!

Our love toward others does not mean that we ignore sin. It does not mean that we must be accepting of every lifestyle. To love means that we genuinely care about the good of others. It means that we value them as highly as ourselves, and that we would give up our own wants, desires, and comfort, to work for the good of others. Part of this means that we need to confront others about their sin because we genuinely care about their souls. But we should do this gently, and never with the intention to attack, but with the goal of restoration.

Love shows itself in two ways: by taking care of others physical needs, and taking care of one's spiritual needs. Jesus helped people physically. He gave them food, and restored their health. But even more importantly, he fulfilled spiritual needs. He brought the Word of God to people, as both law and gospel. He proclaimed the forgiveness of sins and his death on the cross. We too, are to demonstrate our love toward others in both of these ways. When people are in need of food, shelter, money, or whatever else it might be, we are called to aid them insofar as we are able to. We should be concerned about the physical well-being of others. And that does not just mean our own friends, but those who we don't know, or even don't like. Some Christians have the idea that they cannot help with one's physical needs without then using it as an opportunity to immediately begin evangelizing to them. While bringing the gospel to others should certainly be a priority for us, we can't just help people's physical needs as an excuse to preach to them. The one who you have helped will then begin to think that you don't genuinely care about them, and that you weren't really concerned about their needs, but that you just wanted an excuse to evangelize. God calls us to love and serve others. This means that we don't always need to have the ulterior motive of preaching the gospel. Sometimes, when we have opportunity, we can simply help others for the sake of the other person.

Evangelism is, however, also an essential part of the commandment to love. Jesus was not afraid to speak to others about himself, but he did it often. Along with the danger of thinking that we help others *only* so that we can bring the gospel to them, there is also a danger in attending to people's physical needs while ignoring their spiritual ones. People will not repent simply because we give them a free cup of coffee. The gospel must be proclaimed boldly. Our evangelism should always be rooted in the distinction between law and gospel, which helps us to discern in what situation one needs to hear about God's demands in the law, and when they need to hear the gospel. If we encounter someone who is feeling extreme guilt, or someone who is struggling with depression and feeling like life is meaningless, then we should bring them the gospel, and let them know that there is hope in Christ if they would believe. In other circumstances, we might encounter people who live openly sinful lifestyles, and seemingly have no guilt at all about the way in which they are living. These people need to hear God's law.

Christ's Presence in us Helps us to Imitate Him

Our imitation of Christ's life is not something we can do in our own power. In and of ourselves, we will not demonstrate humility. We will not love others, but we will only be concerned about our own desires. It is only through the gracious presence of Christ within is that our hearts can begin to change, and we can begin to imitate our Lord's example. Paul demonstrates this connection between our mystical union with God and the transformation which occurs in our lives:

Since we have such a hope, we are very bold, not like Moses, who would put a veil over his face so that the Israelites might not gaze at the outcome of what was being brought to an end. But their minds were hardened. For to this day, when they read the old covenant, that same veil remains unlifted, because only through Christ is it taken away. Yes, to this day whenever Moses is read a veil lies over their hearts. But when one turns to the Lord, the veil is removed. Now the Lord is the Spirit, and where the Spirit of the Lord is, there is freedom. And we all, with unveiled face, beholding the glory of the Lord, are being transformed into the same image from one degree of glory to another. For this comes from the Lord who is the Spirit. (2 Cor. 3:12-18)

Paul references an event that occurred during the time of Moses. On Mt. Sinai, Moses beheld the glory of God. When experiencing that glory, vestiges of it remained on Moses' own face. When he came down from Mount Sinai, the Israelites could literally see the glory of God which showed on Moses' face. This light was so bright that Moses had to put a veil over his face, to stop the Israelites from hurting their eyes when looking at him.

Paul compares this experience that Moses had with the glory of God to our own experience with God. Paul writes that each of us, with unveiled faces, are "beholding the glory of the Lord." The glory of the Lord is shown in the person and work of Jesus Christ. As we continue to look upon the beautiful message of the gospel, we see God's glory reflected in Christ. And as we look at who Christ is and what Christ has done for us, we become more like him. His glory transforms is into his image. It is only through Christ's work within us, that we can look to him as our example, and walk as he walked.

Resources for Further Reading:

Biermann, Joel D. *A Case for Character: Toward a Lutheran Virtue Ethics*. Minneapolis: Fortress, 2014.

Gerhard, Johann. *Sacred Meditations*. Translated by Wade R. Johnson. Saginaw, MI: Magdeburg, 2011.

Harless, Adolf Von. *A System of Christian Ethics*. Fairfield, IA: Just and Sinner, 2014.

Sartorius, Ernst. *The Doctrine of the Person and Work of Christ*. Fairfield, IA: Just and Sinner, 2014.

Walther, C.F.W. *Selected Sermons*. American Lutheran Classics Vol. 9. Fairfield, IA: Just and Sinner, 2014.

CHAPTER 8

LIVING AS A SINNER-SAINT

People often contrast saints and sinners. We divide people into two classes: those who are holy (saints) and those who are not (sinners). There is no grey area. We are either good *or* evil. I once heard a popular preacher say, "It's impossible to be a sinner and a saint at the same time!" Scripture teaches the exact opposite. All of us who believe are in fact both saints and sinners at the same time.

Being a Saint

The Roman Catholic Church uses the term "saint" to refer to specific individuals who have lived particularly holy lives. These are the people who have followed God in some kind of exceptional manner. We still use this term to refer to particular figures in the history of the church. For example, we talk about St. Paul, St. Peter, or St. Augustine. When speaking in this way, we are using the term "saint" in the colloquial sense, of people who have led particularly exemplary lives.

But Scripture does not use the term saint in this way. Instead, Scripture refers to *all* believers as saints. The tendency to separate saints from sinners is from the human desire to see oneself as better than others. In the middle ages, Christians were divided into two separate groups. First, there were the regular Christians, who lived normal lives, got married, worked normal jobs, etc. The other, or more holy Christians, were those who decided to live lives of celibacy as monastics or priests. Some even divided God's law between these two groups. The commandments given in the Sermon on the Mount, for example, were called the "evangelical councils" that applied solely to those who had taken holy orders. While people don't usually talk in those explicit ways today, there are certain traditions which speak about "radical Christians" as opposed to ordinary Christians, or call some of the less holy Christians "carnal Christians."

This is a total misunderstanding of the Biblical terminology of what constitutes a saint. Before God, there is no differentiation between us. We are all judged by the same law, and are saved by the same gospel. Before God, the law does not differentiate between those who have broken it more or less. The apostle James explains:

For whoever keeps the whole law and yet stumbles in one point, he has become guilty of all. For He who said, "Do not commit adultery," also said, "Do not commit

MURDER." *Now if you do not commit adultery, but do commit murder, you have become a transgressor of the law.* (James 2:20-11)

There is only one thing that God accepts for justification—one hundred percent perfect and complete obedience to his entire law. You cannot plead before God that you haven't broken the whole law, but only certain points. There is no getting off the hook with God. Before God's law, it makes no difference if I am Mother Theresa or Hitler. Either way I have broken it and I am condemned. It is in this sense that each of us is declared to be a total sinner before God's law. *Coram Deo* we cannot talk about some Christians being "better" than others. Here, there is no difference between us.

When Scripture uses the term "saint," it is speaking of this *coram Deo* relationship. Just as we are declared a total sinner under God's law, so we are declared totally saint in the gospel. We are saints, not because of anything that we do, but because of who we are in Christ. A saint is simply "one who is holy." In our own lives, we never measure up to God's righteous standard, and are never in and of ourselves holy. It is Jesus Christ and him alone who is holy. Therefore, the only way that we can ever be truly holy before God is by being *in Christ.* To be a baptized Christian is to be a saint. This is the same as the broad sense of the term sanctification, which refers to the complete holiness we have in Christ.

Saints as Sinners

Those of us who are saints are also sinners. This principle is clear in Scripture. There are some pretty explicit times in which this idea, that we are both saints and sinners, is described. One is from Paul's discussion of the faith of Abraham. He writes:

What then shall we say was gained by Abraham, our forefather according to the flesh? For if Abraham was justified by works, he has something to boast about, but not before God. For what does the Scripture say? "Abraham believed God, and it was counted to him as righteousness." Now to the one who works, his wages are not counted as a gift but as his due. And to the one who does not work but believes in him who justifies the ungodly, his faith is counted as righteousness. (Rom. 4:1-5)

This appears in a discussion of the teaching of justification, that God declares people righteous through faith. He cites one particular verse from Genesis 15 which notes that Abraham was counted as righteous because he believed. What is particularly interesting is that Abraham first came to faith three chapters prior to this verse. In chapter twelve, we are told that Abraham heard the call of God and left paganism to follow him. Even after Abraham had been following God for three chapters, his righteousness was not dependent upon him, but only on the righteousness that God grants through faith. This shows that no matter what kind of piety Abraham had, his status before God was still dependent upon Christ's righteousness rather than himself. What is even more interesting here is that Paul uses Abraham as an example to teach that God "justified the ungodly." Paul calls Abraham ungodly! This was a man who had just left everything he knew to follow the call of God. This is someone who we would look at as a great and holy man, yet he is, according to Paul, ungodly. This shows us that before God's law, even though Abraham was being sanctified, he is still declared to be a sinner. This is why saving righteousness must always come from outside of us. Abraham, like us, was both a saint and a sinner. He was a sinner under God's law, but a saint because of who God declared him to be in Christ.

Another great example of this principle is found in Paul's first letter to the Corinthians. This congregation had several pervasive issues. Paul mentions that people in this church were divided against one another. They had been identifying themselves with particular people instead of with Christ. Some were claiming to be followers of Paul, and others were claiming to be followers of Apollos. These groups divided against one another. Paul writes that this caused strife and jealousy between members (1 Cor.

3:3). Along with these divisions, there is also an instance of sexual immorality in the congregation. There was a member of the congregation who was sleeping with his own stepmother, which Paul notes was seen as evil even by pagans. The other people in the church were doing absolutely nothing about this particular sin. There were also members who had been pursuing lawsuits against one another, and some others had been spending time with prostitutes. The church was a complete mess.

If there was any church in the New Testament which one would think would not have earned the title of "saints," it was the Corinthians church. Paul addresses his letter to the Corinthians by calling them "those sanctified in Christ Jesus, called to be saints" (1 Cor. 1:2). The Corinthians are those who are sanctified, or holy. They are saints. In chapter six, Paul reminds them again of their identity in Christ: "You were washed, you were sanctified, you were justified in the name of the Lord Jesus Christ and by the Spirit of our God" (1 Cor. 6:11). In battling the sin that they had fallen into, Paul points the Corinthians back to their baptismal identity. They could not live in sin, because that is not who they are! They are saints. They are those who are holy in Christ, who have been baptized and had their sins taken away.

Even though you are condemned by God's law, and even when you are in one of those really tough times in your life where you feel like you have some deep sin that you can't overcome, you are a saint. You are not a saint because of anything in yourself, but because you have been baptized into Christ.

Part Saint and Part Sinner

While before God, we are declared to be *fully* sinners under the law and *fully* righteous in the gospel, before the world we are also *partially* saint and *partially* sinner. We are on the path from sinner to saint, as we daily struggle with sin and as we grow in our sanctification. It's not an excuse for us not to try and walk like Christ to just say, "Well, I'm a complete sinner! I can't do anything good anyway, so why even try?" God desires that we would grow in our holiness in this life, and cease from sin. Jesus, when speaking to an adulteress woman confessing her sins pronounces her totally free and forgiven. But he does not leave her there; instead he says, "Go and sin no more" (John 8:11). We are called, as sinner-saints, to battle against our sin nature.

There are some Christian traditions which get this part wrong. The Wesleyan tradition, for example, teaches that Christians can come so far in their sanctification that they will stop sinning. Scripture does not teach this view of sanctification. The Lord's Prayer is the model for prayer for the Christian on this earth in which we ask the Lord to forgive our sins. There is no Christian on this earth who cannot pray the Lord's Prayer, as if he somehow has progressed beyond it. We also see that even the greatest saints in Scripture, those who surely would have achieved this perfect sanctification if it were possible, struggle with sin. Peter denied Christ, Abraham lied to Pharaoh about the identity of his wife, David committed adultery, and Noah got drunk.

There are two aspects to who we are as Christian people. First, there is the old Adam. This is what Scripture refers to as the sinful flesh. This is the sinful part of us which comes from Adam. By birth, sin infects our nature. When the Bible talks about sin, it speaks two ways. First, there are various specific sins. These are specific acts which we do that break God's law. But if we only speak about *sins*, but not about *sin*, then we have missed the problem. Underneath individual sins is the condition of sin. This is called original sin. By birth, because we are born of corrupt and sinful parents, we are sinful. This means that our wants and desires are opposed to God's will. The root of the problem must be dealt with before the fruit of individual sins is taken care of. This is what our regeneration does. As we are born again, we are changed. We are no longer only in the flesh, but we are also in the Spirit.

The second part of who we are is our spiritual nature. When contrasting flesh and spirit we must not think that this means that the body itself is a bad thing. Flesh and bone, and the physical constitution of man are a good thing. Jesus himself still has a human body.

If the human body itself was bad, God would not have created it! Scripture uses these terms symbolically. Flesh refers to that part of us which is sinful, and spirit refers to that part of us which is holy and righteous. According to the spiritual part of us, insofar as we have been renewed, we desire only God's will. We do not want to live in sin, but we want to be obedient to all of the commandments which God gives us.

The relationship between the flesh and the spirit is one of battle. We have these two parts of ourselves that are diametrically opposed to one another. Paul explains the relationship between these two parts of our constitution to the Galatians, writing:

For the desires of the flesh are against the Spirit, and the desires of the Spirit are against the flesh, for these are opposed to each other, to keep you from doing the things you want to do. (Gal. 5:17)

We have two different sets of desires. The flesh desires only sin, but the spirit desires only righteousness. There are times in our lives that we are going to fall deeply into sin. We are going to give in to the desires of the flesh, instead of listening to the spirit. However, when you fall into these kinds of sins, there is going to be a part of you that sincerely desires *not* to do what you are doing! Paul confesses that when he sins, "It is no longer I who do it, but sin that dwells within me" (Rom. 7:20). When you sin, it is not your true self that is sinning.

Who you really are is not your sin nature. Your true self is your spirit, who you have been made in Christ, and who Christ is making you by living in you. The Christian life is a battle until death, because the sinful flesh clings with us as long as were are in this life. When we are in really difficult situations in our lives spiritually, when it seems like we just need to give up, or that we can't do it anymore, we need to remember the words of Paul when describing his own battle with the flesh: "Wretched man that I am! Who will deliver me from this body of death? Thanks be to God through Jesus Christ our Lord" (Rom 7:24)! God gives us the promise that one day, we will be set free from our sinful flesh, and Christ will have the victory.

The Three Functions of the Law

God's law has three different functions in the world. These are often described as the "three uses" of the law. The first use is the *civil* use. This is the place that God's law has in the broader culture and society. This is the role that God's law has in the left hand kingdom. All society and culture needs some kind of law to restrain evil and keep the world in order. People don't steal, for example, because they don't want to get caught. They don't commit adultery because they don't want to make their spouse mad and face the consequences. This law pertains to *civil righteousness,* which is not righteousness in the true sense. It helps people to do outwardly good acts for the benefit of society, but these benefits are not spiritually good and acceptable before God, because they are not done in faith.

The second use of the law, or its primary use, is to show people their sin. This is the *pedagogical* function of the law. This is the use of the law being referred to when we are discussing the contrast between law and gospel. This is the use of the law *coram Deo*. Through the law, we see our inadequacy at keeping it, and come to a knowledge of sin. The Spirit uses the law to convict us of our sins. It is a mirror, showing us who we truly are before God. This use of the law is concerned with *passive righteousness*, because it prepares us for the gospel, wherein we receive the righteousness of Christ on our account.

The third use of the law is its *didactic* use. This means that those of us who have been regenerated, who are justified by faith, who have been put in a right relationship with God, now have the law as a guide. The law informs us what God's good will is for our lives. It tells us how we are to love him and our neighbor. This is concerned with *conforming righteousness*, or sanctification. The law is necessary as a guide for Christians, because if we did not have God's will before us, we would be tempted to make up our own rules according to our sinful nature instead of following God's.

There have been many times in the history of the church where man decided which laws people should follow without actually listening to God's Word.

The Pharisees did this in the New Testament. Instead of being concerned with the weightier matters of the law, namely the intentions of the heart, the Pharisees were concerned with external obedience to rituals. These rituals were often not even explicitly commanded in Scripture. The medieval church did this in Luther's time. The church taught that good works included buying indulgences, kissing relics, and praying to saints. Many Christians today make up their own rules also. Some traditions have strict rules about drinking alcohol. The drinking of alcohol is never condemned as a sin in Scripture, though drunkenness is. I have met many Christians who engaged in openly sinful behavior who claimed that God spoke to their heart, and told them that behavior was ok! This is why we need God's law. Without it, our sinful flesh will make up its own rules. If we did not have the old Adam clinging to us, we would not need to constantly be reminded of God's law, because we have the law written on our hearts (Jer. 31:33). However, since we live this life as both sinners and saints, we need to continue to hear God's will.

All three of these functions of the law apply to Christians. We still need the civil use, because we live in a society which has rules, and due to our sinful flesh, we are tempted to break them. Sometimes we too, even as Christians, need threats of punishment to stop us from doing things that are against God's will. We also continue to need the law in its second function, because we sin each and every day. It is a good and helpful practice for Christians to read through the Ten Commandments each evening. When we do this, we can think back on our day and see where we have fallen short. We might remember that we really didn't love our neighbor very well at work today, or that we had lust in our heart toward someone who is not our spouse. As we do this, we confess our sins to God, and receive his forgiveness. If we don't look at the law to see our shortcomings, we will not continue to see our constant need for Jesus. The third function of the law is also essential for Christians. Luther mentions that we should sing a happy tune, such as the Ten Commandments, when we go off to work. In the morning, as we wake up, it is a good practice to make the sign of the cross over ourselves and remind ourselves of who we are in Christ. We are God's beloved children, freely justified before him. We then, in full assurance of our salvation, should look to God's law as a guidebook for how to handle ourselves at work and with our families. The law helps us to make right decisions as God's people. Ultimately of course, even the third function of the law then reminds us of how we have fallen short of God's will for our lives, bringing us back to the second use, and points us again to the passive righteousness we have in Christ.

The Different Kinds of Sin

As we battle against our sinful flesh in this life, we must learn to recognize the different kinds of sin that we struggle with. Some of these divisions include: sins of omission and sins of commission, willful sins and accidental sins, and sins of thought, word, and deed.

Sin includes both doing things that are condemned in God's law and avoiding doing things which are commanded in his law. There many things which are explicitly prohibited in the law. For example, we are told not to lie. If we choose to lie, we are willfully making the decision to break one of God's commandments. These kinds of sins are rather obvious to us, as we know that we are doing something wrong when we choose to disobey God. These are sins of *commission*. There are other sins, those of *omission*, which might not be as obvious to us. This is when we fail to do something that God has called us to do. Our lives might look pretty good from the outside because we don't steal, we don't commit adultery, and we don't lie very often. But at the same time, we might be sinning constantly by not looking out for the good of our neighbor. If you spend all of your time and money on yourself, you are sinning, because you are not looking out for the good of the neighbor. You are not using your resources as God has called you to.

Some sins are done willfully, and others are done accidentally. There are also some differences between willful sins. For example, you might have planned on watching pornography when your spouse wasn't home for the past week. That is a premeditated willful sin. On the other hand, you might have done that while your spouse was away, not because you had planned on it, but because you came across it online and made a bad decision at that moment. There are also times when we sin accidentally, without even thinking about it. Perhaps my friend really needed help and comfort in a difficult situation. When they told me about it, I wasn't really paying attention to what they were saying, and didn't help them. The next week they confront me about it, and I hadn't actually realized what I had done. We need to confess all of these sins, including those that were not done on purpose, and we must ask for God's help to overcome them.

There are three different ways in which we can sin before God: in thought, word, and deed. We can sin in thought by thinking really mean things about the person who has an office next to us. We might not actually let our thoughts be known to anyone else, as we act nice, and use words which would not convey our real thoughts about the person. We also can sin in word. I might let something slip about how I really don't like that person, and I end up gossiping with others at work. Even though I haven't done anything intentionally mean to that person directly, I have still sinned in the way I talked about them. Finally, we can sin in our deeds. Say that this person I work with has been really bothering me more than usual. Not only do I think evil thoughts about them, and gossip about this person to others, but then I go make up lies to my boss about this person about their bad work habits in hopes that they will get fired from their job.

Before God, each of these things are as sinful as one another. Each condemns us equally before God's law. However, regarding my life in the world, there is an immense difference between thinking something sinful, saying something sinful, and then acting sinfully toward someone. As Christians, we can't say: "Well I already sin in thought, so I might as well just do it in word and deed too!" Instead, we should stop our sinful flesh wherever we can. If you are thinking a bad thought, restrain your flesh so that it doesn't come out of your mouth. If you catch yourself speaking ill of someone, stop your body from doing anything further to sin outwardly. We need to restrain our sinful flesh, and oftentimes it will get the best of us.

Life as a sinner-saint is difficult. The reality of the Christian life is on of struggle, even of battle, between these two natures inside each of us. On the one hand, we have God's Holy Spirit within us, who is at work in us, conforming us to the image of Christ. We have a love for God's law and our neighbor. On the other, we have an evil sinful nature, which hates God's law. It tries to get us to do the opposite of God's will, and enslaves us to sin. But, even though the battle gets difficult, we must not despair, because God promises us that this battle will come to an end, and Christ will be victorious.

Resources for Further Reading:

Cooper, Jordan. *The Great Divide, A Lutheran Evaluation of Reformed Theology.* Eugene, OR: Wipf and Stock, 2015, 180-210.

Kolb, Robert and Charles P. Arand. *The Genius of Luther's Theology: A Wittenberg Way of Thinking for the Contemporary Church.* Grand Rapids: Baker, 2008.

Lange, Lyle W. *Sanctification: Alive in Christ.* Milwaukee: Northwestern, 1999.

Senkbeil, Harold L. *Dying to Live: The Power of Forgiveness.* St. Louis: Concordia, 1994.

CHAPTER 9

LIVING OUT
YOUR VOCATION

We have a tendency in the church to privilege certain callings over others. I remember being in a youth group in high school and feeling like if I wasn't going to go do mission work, then I was not really serving God. True Christians, or at least more mature Christians, have a spiritual profession. Even if you were not actually going to travel overseas, you needed to treat your job as a mission field. If you decided to be a plumber, for example, your primary role in being a plumber was to go to peoples' houses and evangelize to them. Yes you would do what they paid you for, but more importantly, you would then preach the gospel. I recall someone saying that they just felt that they were not given the gift of evangelism, and that they wanted to serve God in a more ordinary way. The youth leader responded to them by saying, "God doesn't call the prepared. He prepares the called." In other words, it doesn't actually matter what gifts it appears God has given you. Either way, you must decide on a spiritual profession.

Vocation: Where God Has Called You

God does not hold one profession over another. Each is necessary in the world. What would the world be like if everyone decided to become missionaries or pastors? Things wouldn't function very well. There would be no one to grow food, no one to make clothing, and no one to clean buildings. Human society is like a body. It has different parts that perform different roles. Though one part might seem less important than another, the body cannot function properly without it. Without farmers, bakers, newscasters, pastors, janitors, or lawyers, the world would not work properly. Everyone has their own unique role to play.

When discussing vocation, we are not talking only about one's career. Your career is only one aspect of your multifaceted life. Along with having a job, you also have a place within your family and community. Even within your family, you have different roles. You might be a mother, and also a daughter, a sister, and an aunt. In each of these positions, you have a different role. The duties you have toward your child will be different toward those you have toward your parents and your siblings. You also have a place in society. You are a citizen, and as a citizen you have duties toward your state. We exist within this complex web of human relationships and vocations.

Scripture does not put unrealistic expectations upon people regarding what they are going to do with their lives. When writing to the Thessalonians, Paul writes: "Aspire to live quietly, and to mind your own affairs, and to work with your hands, as we instructed you" (1 Thess. 4:11). The Thessalonians were working normal jobs, using their hands. And Paul does not tell them to aspire to something greater, but instead he tells them that they should continue doing so. He even mentions that they should "live quietly." The Christian life involves doing what God has called you to do in whatever sphere of life you are working. That does not necessarily mean finding a better career.

God Working in Your Vocations

When you serve in your vocations, it probably seems like you are the one doing all the work. If you go out on your farm and milk your cows, it might seem like God really has nothing to do with what is happening. What would God want to do with milking cows anyway? But vocation is precisely how God works in the world. He works through your own hands and feet.

Martin Luther describes the working of human creatures as "masks of God."[3] God does not work in this world through his bare power. If he wanted to, God could easily work miracles each and every day to control the world. Yet, God has decided that he is going to work in this world through means. This is why God

---

[3] Veith, Gene Edward. "Masks of God: God Works Through Your Vocation, Whatever it May Be" *Lutheran Witness.* St. Louis: Concordia, 2001. http://www.lcms.org/Document.fdoc?src=lcm&id=607

works through the Sacraments. He could, if he chose, save us without any means at all. He could come directly into our souls and change our hearts. But God has decided not to do that. And so God works through regular earthly things. He works through words typed on a page in Holy Scripture. He works through ordinary water to regenerate us. Through two of the most ordinary elements of a meal: bread and wine—he brings us Christ's true body and blood! God is not opposed to creation, but he works in and through creation. This includes us. Just as God is present in bread and wine, the waters of Holy Baptism, and his Word, so he is also present in us. We too are earthly elements through which God works. When the farmer milks his cow, God is milking the cow through him. When the baker is making bread, God is making bread through him.

God both Creates and Preserves

As Christians, we speak often of God as the Creator. When we say this, we are usually talking about the act of God which occurred at the beginning of time. He spoke, and through his Word, all things were created. If we spend all of our time speaking of God's past work of creation, we might be tempted to think that he does not have the same control over his creation today. Perhaps this is just something that God did in the past, and God has no power over what happens in the world currently. This is the belief of deists, who teach that God created the world, but today has nothing to do with it. He leaves it on its own course.

In the Small Catechism, Luther explains the meaning of creation in the following words:

> I believe that God has made me and all creatures; that He has given me my body and soul, eyes, ears, and all my members, my reason and all my senses, and still takes care of them
>
> He also gives me clothing and shoes, food and drink, house and home, wife and children, land, animals, and all I have. He richly and daily provides me with all that I need to support this body and life.[4]

For Luther, creation means not only that God made all things in the past, but that he cares for them now. This is called *providence*. God is concerned with our lives, and with our world. He desires for this world to function in its proper order, and ultimately, of course, for this world to be redeemed. Human vocations are how God does this. God provides us food, not by dropping it miraculously from heaven like he did with the manna in the wilderness, but by working through people who have been given the ability to grow and prepare food. He takes care of our bodies, not usually by miracles, but by using the hands of doctors. He has

---

[4] The Creed, First Article. *Luther's Small Catechism with Explanation.* St. Louis: Concordia, 2006, 15.

gifted doctors with the ability to take care of the health of other people. When we get food, clothing, medicine, or anything else that preserves us in this life, we should remember that God is actually doing these things for us. In the same way, when we serve in our vocations, God is using us to provide for others.

Knowing that God desires us to serve in ordinary vocations, and that he is at work within them, we should strive for excellence in our jobs. Whatever career you have (if you have one), you should spend your time at your job, not simply trying to earn money for yourself, but serving your neighbor. Your career is an opportunity for you to serve God and others. Even if you are working a job that you really don't like, or one that you are not very good at, God is working in and through you. He is using you to bless other people. As Christians we should not be lazy in our careers, but we should work diligently. Christians should be known as those who work the hardest, because we know what's actually happening behind our working.

Your Role in the Family
Every person is part of a family, whether biological or otherwise. And within the family, one usually serves many different functions. All of us have parents, and many have spouses, siblings, and children. With each of those roles come different responsibilities. The New Testament outlines many of the responsibilities in various familial roles.

Wives, submit to your own husbands, as to the Lord. For the husband is the head of the wife even as Christ is the head of the church, his body, and is himself its Savior. Now as the church submits to Christ, so also wives should submit in everything to their husbands. (Eph. 5:22-24)

In our contemporary culture, this statement might seem offensive. Paul argues that in a marriage relationship, there is order. Husbands are the head of the household, and wives are called to submit to them. This does not mean that men are somehow *better* than women, but simply that they have different roles within the family. There is structure in creation in the same way that there is structure within God. There is an order in God, where the Son submits to the Father, and the Spirit to both the Father and the Son. All three persons of the Trinity are equal in dignity, holiness, and essence, but play different roles.

Wives are called to respect their husband within their God-ordained position of leadership. After the fall, the natural order of relationships has been corrupted. Women want to take on the role that God gave to men, and in turn, men then want to abuse their power over women. Both of these actions go against God's intentions in marriage. Men naturally want respect. That's how they are designed. And in turn, women should show respect to their husbands. Obedience here does not mean that a wife needs to do absolutely everything her husband says. The man is not a dictator, but one who is to lovingly make decisions with the aid of his wife.

The apostle Peter teaches the same thing about marriage as Paul, while adding that when the wife is respectful of her husband, and the husband is an unbeliever, she might win him to the faith by her actions. Peter writes that the unbelieving husband "may be won without a word by the conduct of their wives" (1 Pet. 3:1). By treating her husband with respect and patience, she is witnessing to the gospel in her actions. The grace shown to us in Christ can be reflected in our relationships with one another.

Husbands, love your wives, as Christ loved the church and gave himself up for her, that he might sanctify her, having cleansed her by the washing of water with the word, so that he might present the church to himself in splendor, without spot or wrinkle or any such thing, that she might be holy and without blemish. In the same way husbands should love their wives as their own bodies. He who loves his wife loves himself. For no one ever hated his own flesh, but nourishes and cherishes it, just as Christ does the church, because we are members of his body. (Eph. 5:25-30)

While the role of the wife remains the most controversial in this passage, the man's role is much more difficult. Husbands are called to love their wives in the same way that Christ loves the church. They are to love their wives to such an extent that they would give their own lives for the sake of their spouse. This is quite a difficult calling! In a proper functioning relationship, the husband will make all of his decisions for the good of his wife, as he considers her interest more than his own. Within this context, the wife submits to her husband, knowing that his decisions have her best interest in mind.

Christian couples should model this kind of relationship, even though both spouses will fall short. Husbands should make every effort to make all of their decisions for the good of their wife, in light of the love which Christ has for his church. In turn, the wife should respect her husband and his decisions, even when she does not necessarily agree with them. If a Christian is in a marriage with an unbeliever, their actions toward a spouse can be an opportunity to witness to the love of Christ. The husband should love his wife, whether she deserves it or not; the wife should respect her husband, whether he deserves it or not.

Children, obey your parents in the Lord, for this is right. "Honor your father and mother" (this is the first commandment with a promise), "that it may go well with you and that you may live long in the land." Fathers, do not provoke your children to anger, but bring them up in the discipline and instruction of the Lord. (Eph. 6:1-4)

Whether or not one is married, everyone has parents. The relationship between a parent and child is one of the most important ones in life. How your parents treat you, and what they teach you as a child is going to impact you the rest of your life. We are all called to honor our parents, which is the fourth commandment. As children, we are to respect them as authorities who God has placed over us. We are called to submit to them and show them respect, whether or not we deem the demand or punishment unfair. When we show disrespect to our parents, we show disrespect to God who placed them over us.

There are several duties placed on parents here as well. We are called not to provoke our children to anger. God does not call parents to be harsh. This can end with children simply becoming bitter against us, or turning away from what we have taught them. Parents, on the other hand, are not to simply let their children do whatever they want without any attempt to discipline them. We are called, as parents, to instruct our children in the fear and admonition of the Lord.

Oftentimes, I have found that parents neglect their spiritual duty. Instead, they leave it to the pastor and the Sunday school teacher to instruct them in the Christian faith. When parents do this, they are essentially telling their children that faith does not matter in the home. It only matters on Sunday mornings. It is primarily the duty of the parent, not the pastor, to raise their child in the faith. It is the parents who the child spends their entire week with. Many parents also don't make their children attend church, leaving it up to the decision of their own child. This is a gross neglect of one's primary duty as a parent! Do you allow your child to make similar decisions about whether or not they will attend school, or join a gang, or do drugs? Of course not! Then why are we so comfortable allowing our children to make a decision which might destroy their soul? We must raise our children in the faith and place this at the center of our home life.

Bondservants, obey your earthly masters with fear and trembling, with a sincere heart, as you would Christ, not by the way of eye-service, as people-pleasers, but as bondservants of Christ, doing the will of God from the heart, rendering service with a good will as to the Lord and not to man, knowing that whatever good anyone does, this he will receive back from the Lord, whether he is a bondservant or is free. Masters, do the same to them, and stop your threatening, knowing that he who is both their Master and yours is in heaven, and that there is no partiality with him. (Eph. 6:5-9)

This particular instruction is written with slaves and masters in mind. Now, this immediately raises the question of the validity of slavery, the relationship between Roman slavery in the first century and the abusive and abhorrent system of slavery in early American history. These issues are complex, and this book is not a place where those questions can be answered. For our purposes here, we will simply note that the relationship being described here is one of a worker, and someone who has hired and pays that worker. Thus the instructions here show us something about the relationships we have in the workplace.

Bondservants are called to obey their masters with "fear and trembling," and serve them in the same manner that they would serve Christ himself. It is quite a difficult thing to imagine treating our bosses as if we were talking to Christ himself. But God has placed these people over us, so that we might obey them. There are no qualifications here as to how good of a person we work for. And the most difficult thing is that Paul says that we are to obey them "from the heart." Much of the time we probably only perform well under coercion. We want to make sure we keep our job, or that we get a raise. But ultimately, we should not work for earthly rewards. We should work hard because God has called us to, and because we have an opportunity to serve our neighbors in that position.

Masters are given difficult admonitions as well in this text. Paul writes that they should "do the same to them." Those who are in charge of other workers are also to treat their workers as they would treat Christ himself. He also notes that they should stop their threatening. If we are in a position of authority, we are called not to abuse that position, but to treat others with grace and kindness, just as Christ has treated us. While there are differences in the world in terms of our positions, whether rich or poor, master or slave, male or female, there is no difference before God who shows "no partiality." We are all saved the same way.

The Christian life is not about a monastic retreat into the desert, nor is it necessarily about giving up everything to serve as a missionary overseas. The Christian life is about living in the ordinary world. We are called to live in families, careers, and communities, just as everyone else is. But behind all that we do in these vocations, we recognize that God is at work in us and through us. We should view these vocations as a joy and a privilege, as a place where God himself has chosen to work through us!

Resources for Further Reading:

Veith, Gene E. *God at Work: Your Christian Vocation in all of Life.* Crossway, 2011.

_____. Family Vocation: God's Calling in Marriage, Parenting, and Childhood. Wheaton, IL: Crossway, 2012.

_____. *Working for our Neighbor: A Lutheran Primer on Vocation, Economics, and Ordinary Life.* Wheaton, IL: Christian's Library, 2016.

Wingren, Gustaf. *Luther on Vocation.* Translated by Carl C. Rasmussen. Philadelphia: Muhlenberg, 1957.

CHAPTER 10

LITURGICAL LIFE

What comes to mind when you hear the word "liturgy?" For many, this is viewed as rote formalism. Liturgical worship is without heart or spirit. Instead, liturgy is for dead churches without a vital faith. This perception, however, could not be farther from the truth! The liturgy of the church is not empty, nor is it simply a compilation of various human traditions. In the liturgy, the words and teachings of Scripture come alive as God gives his gifts to his people.

There is a very specific pattern to a liturgical worship service, and there is a reason for this structure. The liturgy is a conversation between God and man. God acts as a loving giver of salvation, and man as the grateful recipient of that salvation. This establishes the pattern of God giving, man receiving, and then the congregation giving thanks and praise to God in light of these gifts.

If you are sitting in an old church with a small number of congregants, a pastor who can't preach very well, and an organist who never learned how to play properly, you probably don't recognize that anything special is happening. Yet, in that worship service, something profound is going on behind the scenes. Heaven and earth are joining together. You are not only worshipping with the saints in that church, but with all of the saints and angels in heaven and on earth! There is an invisible reality of the communion of saints which is at work.

Liturgical Worship in Scripture

Any treatment of the Christian life must approach the topic of worship, because worship of God is at the center of one's life of faith. Because worship is a topic which must be addressed, the mode and manner of worship should be dealt with. Christians disagree on the issue of exactly how the Lord desires to be worshipped. Many in the Anabaptist tradition have services which are as plain as possible, eschewing any form of art and ornamentation. Those who are within the Reformed tradition believe that God sets strict parameters around what constitutes worship in the New Testament. Some in this tradition argue that no human written hymns should be used in worship, and argues against the use of instruments. Because of these disagreements, we must ultimately look at worship in Scripture.

It might be surprising that the book of the New Testament which speaks the most often about worship is the Revelation of St. John. We often think of the

Apocalypse simply as a collection of end time prophecies, but it is actually a book about worship. In between his visions regarding the history of the world, John describes worship in heaven before the throne of God. When looking at some of the details of this heavenly worship, it begins to look a lot like a liturgical worship service! Remember, in worship, heaven and earth become one. If this is true, then our worship here should reflect worship in heaven.

Throughout the book of Revelation, the angels and saints are said to speak or sing certain phrases in a particular pattern. In Revelation 4:8, for example, we read that the living creatures recite the phrase, "Holy, holy, holy is the Lord God almighty, who was and is and is to come!" day and night. Some Christians believe that repetitious phrases are meaningless, and that memorized prayers should not be said. However, these creatures in heaven *only* recite memorized words of praise. It is true that some people come to a worship service, recite the necessary words, and then leave without giving any thought to what just happened. But when we understand what is actually happening in worship, that heaven and earth come together, and that God gives us salvation, we should speak and sing the liturgy with great joy! This is our opportunity to praise the Lord who saved us! We should put our whole heart before God in the worship service.

Several aspects of a liturgical service remind us of this heavenly reality behind Christian worship. In heaven, God's saints are washed in white robes (Rev. 4:4). The pastor, and others helping during the service, wear white robes just as we all will wear in heaven, as we are washed in the blood of the Lamb! The pastor's vestments are a picture of the gospel. Worship in heaven also has an altar, candles, and incense (Rev. 8:3). These elements are reflected in worship on earth. The saints and angels also have certain postures, like bowing, that happen at certain times during the heavenly worship service (Rev. 4:10-11). Many of the songs sung in worship are also based on these heavenly worship songs in Revelation.

In our modern context, we often think about our lives of faith as an individual and personal affair. I've heard people say that their spiritual life is only about, "me, my Bible, and Jesus." They think that somehow they don't have any need for corporate worship, or with their brothers and sisters in Christ. Through liturgical worship, we come to the reality that the Christian life is not just about us. It's about all of God's people. We are part of the family of God. All who have been baptized are also part of that family. We have millions of brothers and sisters in this family all around the world! As we sing and praise the Lord, these saints do so with us. The angels and saints in glory also sing and praise the Lamb alongside of us!

Holy Absolution

One of the most important aspects of the worship service within the Lutheran tradition is the opening practice of confession and absolution. When gathered together in worship before the throne of God, the people of God recognize that they cannot stand before him in their own righteousness. Like the prophet Isaiah, we see God's holiness and recognize our own unholiness (Isaiah 6:5). This leads to a corporate confession of sins by the Christian congregation. The people of God speak together, acknowledging that they have sinned against the Triune God in "thought, word, and deed." There is a time here for each person to silently consider the various ways in which sin has been committed in the previous week. The law convicts us, not only as individuals, but also as a congregation.

Following this confession of sins, the pastor proclaims the forgiveness of sins through a word of absolution. In Scripture, cleansing is necessary for anyone to stand in God's presence. In the book of Isaiah, the prophet is brought into the throne room of God, and confesses his sins. God then offers him cleansing from his sin by sending an angel to place a burning coal on Isaiah's lips (Isaiah 6:6-7). After he had been cleansed from his iniquity, he was then able to stand before the throne of God without any fear of punishment. The absolution, in the worship service, is like this burning coal. In church, we enter into the house of God, and acknowledge that we are unworthy to do so. God then offers us healing, cleansing, and forgiveness through the declaration of the pastor.

The absolution is a means by which forgiveness is brought from God to his people. While standing in the sanctuary before the presence of God, the minister declares, "I forgive you all of your sins in the name of the Father, the Son, and of the Holy Spirit." To many Christians, such a statement may seem confusing, or even blasphemous! How can this man forgive my sins? Isn't this *God's* role? Scripture is clear, however, that this is something which can be done by means of God's people. There are two passages which are particularly emphatic on this point.

"If you forgive the sins of any, they are forgiven them; if you withhold forgiveness from any, it is withheld." (John 20:23)

"I will give you the keys of the kingdom of heaven, and whatever you bind on earth shall be bound in heaven, and whatever you loose on earth shall be loosed in heaven." (Matt. 16:19)

In the first passage, Jesus speaks to his disciples following the resurrection as he gives them guidance surrounding the building up of the church after Christ's ascension. In the second, Jesus gives a commandment to Peter prior to his death and resurrection. In both instances, Christ is explicit that the disciples are called to forgive, or loosen, sins.

The ability of the church to absolve sins is often referred to as the "power of the keys," due to Jesus' description in Matthew 16 of the keys of the kingdom of heaven given to Peter and then to the rest of the disciples (Matt. 18:18). These keys are given, not just to specific individuals, but to the church. When the pastor declares "I forgive you," he is not acting on his own power or authority. He is speaking with the authority of Christ. Think back to the story of Isaiah in the throne room of God. When receiving cleansing, God uses an angel to bring the burning coal to Isaiah. There is nothing about even a creature as majestic as an angel which would allow him to forgive sins in his own power. Yet, God chose to use him as an instrument to bring cleansing and healing to Isaiah. In the same way, God uses the pastor as his instrument to proclaim forgiveness to the congregation. When the pastor declares, "I forgive you," it is as if Christ himself is standing before you speaking these words to you.

Absolution is a great comfort to the people of God. While it is a great blessing to remember the promises of Christ in one's own mind, or encounter them while reading Scripture, there is something unique about hearing that forgiveness proclaimed from the outside. We are often entrapped by our subjective feelings of guilt, unable to convince ourselves that Christ's forgiveness is really good enough even to cover our worst sins. When we hear this forgiveness come from someone else, we have something concrete that we can cling to. We can *know* that this forgiveness is indeed for us. Absolution becomes the fuel that keeps us going as we walk with Christ. We strive for obedience and conformity to the image of Christ only in view of the absolution that is continually proclaimed to us.

The Lord's Supper

The culminating act of the church's liturgical life is Holy Communion. Through this sacrament, God gives his people Christ's true body and blood for the forgiveness of sins. This sacrament preserves us in faith, and strengthens our union with Christ. The Supper is also an act which connects us to our fellow believers in Christ, as we are united to the entire family of God, through a reception of Christ himself.

In many contemporary churches, the Supper is viewed, not as a sacrament, but an act of human memorial. Just like in baptism, the question must be asked—whose work is the Lord's Supper? Is it something that the human creature offers to God, or is it a divine gift from the Creator to his people? Many churches answer this question with the former option. In Scripture, however, the Supper is not a human act. It is an offering from God to man, wherein the human person simply acts as a receiver.

Holy Baptism constitutes the beginning of one's relationship to God. Through this sacrament, one is united to Christ and receives his benefits. As was established previously, this beginning of the life of faith is the result of pure grace. The Lord's Supper, in contrast to baptism, is a sacrament that is continually received. The question of how one views the Supper is vital to understanding the Christian life. If one sees it as a human act toward God, one will view the relationship that the creature has with God as one where the human acts to preserve the relationship that one has with God. If the Lord's Supper is, however, a word of gospel, then it demonstrates that the gospel is the continual means by which the Christian's life is established. Christian life is all about grace, from beginning to end.

Christians have debated the meaning of the Lord's Supper for many centuries. At the time of the Reformation, Martin Luther and the Swiss reformer Ulrich Zwingli refused Christian fellowship with one another after an extensive debate about this issue. Zwingli argued that the Lord's Supper was a symbol of Christ's body and blood, but Martin Luther defended the notion that Christ is truly present in this meal. Christ offers his real body and real blood to the people of God!

There are two primary places in Scripture where we are told about the Lord's Supper. The first is in the narratives of the Last Supper in the Gospels. These include what are often known as the "words of institution." Matthew writes:

Now as they were eating, Jesus took bread, and after blessing it broke it and gave it to the disciples, and said, "Take, eat; this is my body." And he took a cup, and when he had given thanks he gave it to them, saying, "Drink of it, all of you, for this is my blood of the covenant, which is poured out for many for the forgiveness of sins. I tell you I will not drink again of this fruit of the vine until that day when I drink it new with you in my Father's kingdom." (Matt. 26:26-29)

When Jesus gives the disciples the bread, he says: "This *is* my body." He does not say "this represents my body" or "this symbolizes my body." Jesus teaches us that when we partake of the Lord Supper, we receive his actual body! It is his gift to us.

It is important that Jesus gives the first Lord's Supper during the time of Passover. During Passover, the Jews ate a lamb in remembrance of the lambs that were killed during the Exodus. These lambs had their blood spread upon the doorposts of God's people, and this allowed the angel of death to pass over them. Christ is the true Passover lamb, and through his blood, we are set free from death. In the same way that during the remembrance of the Passover, the Jews again ate a lamb, as we remember Jesus' sacrifice, we partake of the true Lamb of God in that meal! It is more than just a symbol.

In the book of 1 Corinthians, Paul speaks to a congregation that took advantage of God's gifts. While partaking of the Lord's Supper, some people were drinking so much wine that they got drunk. They were also divided against one another, but the Supper is supposed to be a sacrament of unity and peace! Paul responds to them by reminding them of the importance of the Lord's Supper. He explains with the following words:

The cup of blessing that we bless, is it not a participation in the blood of Christ? The bread that we break, is it not a participation in the body of Christ? (1 Cor. 10:16)

According to Paul, the importance of Holy Communion is that through it we participate ("commune" in some translations) in the body and blood of Christ. This is more than just a symbolic act. This is why Paul takes sin against the Lord's Supper so seriously. He writes that those who sin at the table are sinning against "the body and blood of the Lord" (1 Cor. 11:27). This is not just a sin against a symbol!

It is important that we understand the truth of what is happening during the Lord's Supper, because we begin to see how important Holy Communion actually is in the Christian life. Like Baptism, and God's Word, the Lord's Supper is God's gift to us! It is a blessing, and we should receive it in joy. Through this great gift, we commune with our Savior!

Daily Liturgical Life

If you think about liturgy, you probably think about worship on Sunday morning. When gathered with all of the saints in our congregations, we pray together, hear Scripture together, and sing with one another. While these acts of corporate worship are essential for our lives in Christ, we can incorporate liturgical spirituality in everyday life.

One of the ways in which Christians have lived a liturgical life daily is by praying at certain times each day. As early as the book of Acts, Christians designated certain times of day to pray specific prayers (Acts 3:1). This was a common practice in Judaism, and Christians took it from their predecessors. In the early church, this often happened at every third hour: 6 am, 9 am, 12 pm, 3 pm, 6 pm, and 9 pm. These times marked a variety of periods during the typical day in ancient Roman life, and Christians used these opportunities to spend time in prayer. Obviously, for people in ordinary jobs, it is not necessarily possible to take time at each of these hours and spend an extensive amount of time in prayer. Monks used each of these hours to pray and sing to God, but for those of us who are unable to do so, we can pray each morning and evening.

Along with prayer during these specific hours in the day, Christians have often used these times to sing, chant, or pray Psalms. God gave his church a book of songs and prayers which, unfortunately, we don't often take advantage of. The Psalms should be the daily songs of God's people. There are books of Psalms, readings, and prayers which are to be read each day at these times. One does not have to necessarily follow these precise patterns, but they can help one to remain disciplined in continual Scripture reading and prayer. There are also daily lectionaries, which contain a variety of Scripture readings for each day of the week, which follow the themes of the church year. Another helpful practice is to read the Scripture readings for the following Sunday each day prior to the Divine Service. This allows for in-depth reading and meditation of specific Scripture passages each day.

Alongside of one's personal time of prayer, if one lives with family, it is a blessing for families to develop a pattern of worship together. While no formal constraints are given in Scripture regarding exactly what mode this should take, there are a number of beneficial ways in which this can be done. A family can take a specific time each morning or evening (both, if possible) to pray, read Scripture, and sing. Like in personal times of devotional, this can incorporate lectionary readings, Psalms, and memorized and spontaneous prayer. For young children, books of Bible stories for kids are a beneficial way of teaching the major portions of Scripture. Martin Luther includes two prayers in his Small Catechism which are also useful in family worship; one is for morning, and the other is for evening. One can also pray the Lord's Prayer, and explain an aspect of this prayer to one's children each day.

The Church Calendar

The church, throughout its existence, has developed a particular calendar. Throughout the year, there are certain themes which are emphasized at different points in the year, which aid in personal devotion and corporate worship. As winter begins, the church enters into Advent, which is the first season of the year. Christians, at this time, look forward with both repentance and hope toward the Christmas celebration. This is followed by twelve days of celebrating Christ's birth at Christmas, and then Epiphany. After a time in Epiphany season, the church enters into to the season of Lent, which is a time for the church to focus on the necessity of repentance, and the seriousness of sin against God. Following this time is Holy Week, which includes services on Maundy Thursday, Good Friday, and Easter. This is then followed by Pentecost, Holy Trinity, and then Reformation and All Saints days in the fall. Each of the seasons gives us a unique opportunity to emphasize particular important aspects of the Christian faith, and can guide us in our spiritual disciplines. In particular, Lent is a season in which many Christians choose to observe fasts, and take up new spiritual disciplines.

Though the New Testament does not tell us exactly how often, or exactly when, fasting is supposed to occur, Jesus is clear that fasting is a regular part of the Christian life (Matt. 6:16). Through fasting, Christians deprive themselves of physical food, so that they can rely on the spiritual food that God gives through his Word. This practice often accompanies a time of repentance over sin. Seasons of the church year like Lent allow Christians to participate in the act of fasting together, and we share a special bond with our fellow-believers as we commit to this spiritual discipline together. Fasting is also a common practice prior to taking Holy Communion, so that one might be prepared for the glorious meal of Christ's true body and blood. Fasting is never to be done on Sundays or on feast days during the year, because rather than mourning, these days are focused on celebration.

There is no specific pattern of liturgical practice commanded in Scripture, but participating in the liturgical life of the church through corporate worship, the church calendar, fasting, family worship, and lectionary readings is an extremely important aspect of the Christian life. Through liturgy, we are able to worship together with all of God's saints, not only in our own congregations, but with those gathered under the Triune God throughout this world. We also learn to incorporate worship in our daily lives as we set aside regular time for prayer, reading, and fasting.

Resources for Further Reading:

Brunner, Peter. *Worship in the Name of Jesus.* Translated by M.H. Bertram. St. Louis: Concordia, 1968.

Pfatteicher, Philip H and Carlos R. Messerli. *Manual on the Liturgy: Lutheran Book of Worship.* Minneapolis: Augsburg, 1979.

Precht, Fred L. *Lutheran Worship: History and Practice.* St. Louis: Concordia, 1993.

Reed, Luther. *The Lutheran Liturgy: A Study of the Common Liturgy of the Lutheran Church in America.* Philadelphia: Fortress, 1947.

CONCLUSION

Throughout this work, we have been discussing what it means to live as one who has been baptized into Christ. The life of God's child is one that is lived day by day, as we continually look to God's law for guidance, as well as so that we might see where we have fallen short. Each day we cling to God's promises of grace and forgiveness as we fall continually fail in our attempts to obey his will. The Christian life is a struggle. We battle against our sinful nature, and sometimes that sinful nature wins. Thankfully, this struggle does not last forever, but God has promised that one day, it will come to an end.

The Christian Life and Last Things

Our lives in Christ always live in view of the end of all things. When Christ returns, the shape of the Christian life will drastically change. At this time, we will no longer have a sinful nature. The old Adam that clings to us will be put to death. The sorrows, struggles, temptations, and sins that characterize our life now will no longer be present. In our lives now, we press toward that future in hope.

Every element of the Christian life is eschatological. This term "eschatology" means "last things." This means that the entire life of the baptized is lived in view of the end, when Jesus returns for his people. We live with the full hope and assurance that on the last day, Christ will have the victory, and we will share in that victory with him. This gives us great joy and assurance as we walk with Jesus day by day. It is common to get discouraged by failure that often accompanies our life in Christ. Yet, we should never let despair overwhelm us, because the promise of eternal life always stands in front of us as a sure and certain hope.

In Holy Baptism, we are made new creatures. This means that we have, through the Sacrament, entered in some sense into the reality of the new heavens and new earth, even now. The gospel, as it is proclaimed to us in preaching, through Scripture, and in Holy Absolution, is, again, a word that brings us out of the old sinful creation into God's new creation. The Lord's Supper, similarly, brings us a taste of the new creation. The feast that we share in the church with Christ is a picture of the final feast that we will all partake in when Jesus returns for his bride. In worship, the church on earth and the church in heaven join with one another in praise before the throne of the Lamb.

Conclusion

It is one thing to simply read and study these various aspects of the Christian life, but it is another to put them into action and live it out. It is my hope that the truths talked about in these pages will not simply remain ideas in one's head, but that they might be lived by those reading this book. May God grant us the grace to remain in this life of faith as we continue to receive his gifts, in light of the promise of eternal life with Christ and his bride.

BIBLIOGRAPHY

Arand, Charles. "Two Kinds of Righteousness as a Framework for Law and Gospel in the Apology." *Lutheran Quarterly* XV/4 (2001): 417-39.

Arand, Charles P. and Joel Biermann. "Why the Two Kinds of Righteousness?" *Concordia Journal* 33/2 (2007) 116-135.

Biermann, Joel D. *A Case for Character: Toward a Lutheran Virtue Ethics.* Minneapolis: Fortress, 2014.

Brunner, Peter. *Worship in the Name of Jesus.* Translated by M.H. Bertram. St. Louis: Concordia, 1968.

Cooper, Jordan. *Christification: A Lutheran Approach to Theosis.* Eugene, OR: Wipf & Stock, 2014.

_____. *The Great Divide, A Lutheran Evaluation of Reformed Theology.* Eugene, OR: Wipf and Stock, 2015.

Das, A. Andrew. *Baptized into God's Family: The Doctrine of Infant Baptism for Today.* Milwaukee: Northwestern, 1997.

Deutschlander, Daniel M. *Civil Government: God's Other Kingdom.* Milwaukee: Northwestern, 1998.

Dobberstein, Leroy A. *Law and Gospel: Bad News-Good News.* Milwaukee: Northwestern, 1996.

Gerberding, George Henry. *The Way of Salvation in the Lutheran Church.* American Lutheran Classics Vol. 1. Fairfield, IA: Just and Sinner, 2013.

Gerhard, Johann. *Sacred Meditations.* Translated by Wade R. Johnson. Saginaw, MI: Magdeburg, 2011.

Giertz, Bo. *The Hammer of God.* Minneapolis: Augsburg, 2005.

Gregory of Nazianzus. "Epistle 101: Critique of Apollinarius and Apollinarianism," *Early Church Texts.*http://www.earlychurchtexts.com/public/gregory ofnaz_critique_of_apolliniarianism.htm

Harless, Adolf Von. *A System of Christian Ethics.* Fairfield, IA: Just and Sinner, 2014.

Hecht, Bill. *Two Wars We Must Not Lose: What Christians Need to Know About Radical Islamists, Radical Secularists, and Why We Can't Leave the Battle Up to Our Divided Government.* Fort Wayne: Concordia Seminary, 2012.

Heiser, James D. and Jerald Dulas. *The One True God, the Two Kingdoms, and the Three Estates.* Malone, TX: Repristination, 2011.

Jacobs, Henry Eyster. *A Summary of the Christian Faith.* American Lutheran Classics Volume 6 Part I. Fairfield, IA: Just and Sinner, 2014, 273-312.

————————. *Elements of Religion.* American Lutheran Classics Volume 5. Fairfield, IA: Just and Sinner, 2013, 199-209.

Kolb, Robert. "Luther on the Two Kinds of Righteousness; Reflections on His Two-Dimensional Definition of Humanity at the Heart of His Theology." *Lutheran Quarterly* XIII/4 (1999): 449-66.

Kolb, Robert and Charles P. Arand. *The Genius of Luther's Theology: A Wittenberg Way of Thinking for the Contemporary Church.* Grand Rapids: Baker, 2008.

Lange, Lyle W. *Sanctification: Alive in Christ.* Milwaukee: Northwestern, 1999.

Luther, Martin. *Galatians.* Crossway Classic Commentaries. Edited by J.I. Packer and Allister McGrath. Wheaton, IL: Crossway, 1998.

_____. *Luther's Small Catechism with Explanation*. St. Louis: Concordia, 2006

Menuge, Angus L. (Editor). *Christ and Culture in Dialogue: Constructive Themes and Practical Applications*. St. Louis: Concordia, 1999.

Molstad, John A. *Predestination: Chosen in Christ*. Milwaukee: Northwestern, 1997

Mueller, Steven P. *Called to Believe, Teach, and Confess: An Introduction to Doctrinal Theology*. Eugene: Wipf & Stock, 2005, 329-346.

Mueller, Wayne D. *Justification: How God Forgives*. Milwaukee: Northwestern, 2002.

Pfatteicher, Philip H and Carlos R. Messerli. *Manual on the Liturgy: Lutheran Book of Worship*. Minneapolis: Augsburg, 1979.

Precht, Fred L. *Lutheran Worship: History and Practice*. St. Louis: Concordia, 1993.

Reed, Luther. *The Lutheran Liturgy: A Study of the Common Liturgy of the Lutheran Church in America*. Philadelphia: Fortress, 1947.

Remensnyder, Junius M. *American Lutheran Classics Volume 8*. Fairfield, IA: Just and Sinner, 2014, 27-32.

Saarnivaara, Uuras *Scriptural Baptism: a Dialog Between John Bapstead and Martin Childfont*. New York: Vantage Press, 1953.

Sartorius, Ernst. *The Doctrine of the Person and Work of Christ*. Fairfield, IA: Just and Sinner, 2014.

Scaer, David P. *Baptism*. Confessional Lutheran Dogmatics Vol. XI. St. Louis: Luther Academy, 1999.

Senkbeil, Harold L. *Dying to Live: The Power of Forgiveness*. St. Louis: Concordia, 1994.

Veith, Gene E. *God at Work: Your Christian Vocation in all of Life*. Crossway, 2011.

_____. Family Vocation: God's Calling in Marriage, Parenting, and Childhood. Wheaton, IL: Crossway, 2012.

_____. "Masks of God: God Works Through Your Vocation, Whatever it May Be" *Lutheran Witness*. St. Louis: Concordia, 2001. http://www.lcms.org/Document.fdoc?src=lcm&id=607

_____. *Working for our Neighbor: A Lutheran Primer on Vocation, Economics, and Ordinary Life*. Wheaton, IL: Christian's Library, 2016.

Voigt, A.G. *Biblical Dogmatics*. American Lutheran Classics Volume 3. Fairfield, IA: Just and Sinner, 2013.

Walther, C.F.W. and Walter C. Pieper. *God's No and God's Yes*. St. Louis: Concordia, 1973.

Walther, C.F.W. *The Proper Distinction Between Law and Gospel*. Translated by C.H. Dau. Fairfield, IA: Just and Sinner, 2014.

_____. *Selected Sermons*. American Lutheran Classics Vol. 9. Fairfield, IA: Just and Sinner, 2014.

Wingren, Gustaf. *Luther on Vocation*. Translated by Carl C. Rasmussen. Philadelphia: Muhlenberg, 1957.

Wright, William J. Martin *Luther's Understanding of God's Two Kingdoms: A Response to the Challenge of Skepticism*. Grand Rapids: Baker, 2010.

Also available from Just and Sinner Publications:

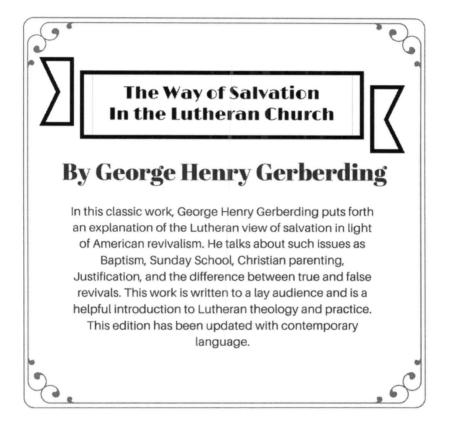

This and more are available at
www.JustandSinnerPublishing.com

Made in the USA
Columbia, SC
03 April 2022

58453516R00098